Thank you...

... for purchasing this copy of Reading for Literacy for ages 5-7. We hope that you find our worksheets, teachers' notes and display materials helpful as part of your programme of literacy activities.

Please note that photocopies can only be made for use by the purchasing institution. Supplying copies to other schools, institutions or individuals breaches the copyright licence. Thank you for your help in this.

This Reading for Literacy book is part of our growing range of educational titles. Most of our books are individual workbooks but, due to popular demand, we are now introducing a greater number of photocopiable titles especially for teachers. You may like to look out for:

READING FOR LITERACY for Reception
and for ages 5-7, 7-8, 8-9, 9-10, 10-11

WRITING FOR LITERACY for ages 5-7, 7-8, 8-9, 9-10, 10-11

SPELLING FOR LITERACY for ages 5-7, 7-8, 8-9, 9-10, 10-11

NUMERACY TODAY for ages 5-7, 7-9, 9-11

HOMEWORK TODAY for ages 7-8, 8-9, 9-10, 10-11

BEST HANDWRITING for ages 7-11

To find details of our other publications, please visit our website: www.acblack.com

ABOUT THIS BOOK

As with all our photocopiable resource books we have kept the teachers' notes to a minimum as we are well aware that teachers will use their own professionalism in using our materials.

At the start of each Unit we list some of the National Literacy Strategy Objectives that the Unit may cover. We are grateful to the Department for Education and Skills for their permission to quote the Objectives.

Some of the Units are linked to others as indicated by their titles.

Many Units feature reading activities that can be undertaken individually or in a small group situation, alongside the teacher or support assistant.

Some Units could be copied onto Overhead Projector Transparencies for use with a large group or the whole class.

The Units vary in their level of difficulty and teachers will match Units to the ability levels of the pupils in their classes.

Most Units are two pages long. All of them provide worthwhile activities as well as useful practice for tests.

The final Unit for Year 2 is a six page Assessment Unit. It includes teachers' notes (Sheet A) and an assessment sheet (Sheet B) to record pupils' reading of the majority of the High Frequency Words for Key Stage One. Sheets C and D contain a story within which these words are set and Sheets E and F feature comprehension questions and practice of alphabetical order.

Extracts from the National Literacy Strategy Framework for Teaching, © Crown copyright 1998, reproduced by kind permission of the Department for Education and Skills.

Contents ...

Year 1   TERM 1

Unit 1	A	The Castle
	B	Sal and Taz (1)

Terms 1/2/3 Objective 1   Word level skills through shared & guided reading.

Unit 2	A	Rhyming Words
	B	Rhyming Words

Terms 1/2/3 Objective 2   Predicting unfamiliar words.

Unit 3	A	Common Colour Words
	B	Days of the Week

Terms 1/2/3 Objective 2   Predicting unfamiliar words.

Unit 4	A	Joey's Day Out
	B	Joey's Day Out

Terms 1/2/3 Objective 2   Predicting unfamiliar words.

Unit 5	A	The Gingerbread Man
	B	The Gingerbread Man

Objective 4   Read simple familiar stories.

Unit 6	A	The Walk
	B	The Walk

Objective 5   Story settings.

Unit 7	A	Labels and Captions
	B	Labels and Captions

Objective 12 To read and use captions.

Unit 8	A	Labelling Pictures (House)
	B	Labelling Pictures (Garden)

Objective 12 To read and use captions.

Unit 9	A	The House to Finish
	B	Illustrating and Labelling a House

Objective 13 Read and follow simple instructions.

TERM 2

Unit 10	A	My Day
	B	My Day

Objective 4   To retell stories

Unit 11	A	Taz and Sal Story (2)
	B	Taz and Sal Story (2)

Objective 7   Reasons for, or causes of, incidents in stories.

Unit 12	A	Finish the Picture (Man)
	B	Finish the Picture (Woman)

Objective 8   Appearance, behaviour and qualities of characters.

Unit 13	A	Humpty Dumpty
	B	Jack and Jill

Objective 8   Appearance, behaviour and qualities of characters.

Unit 14	A	Nursery Rhymes
	B	Action Rhymes

Objective 11 Learn and recite poems and rhymes.

Unit 15	A	A Bear Tale (Fiction)
	B	Bears (Non-Fiction)

Objective 17 Fiction and non-fiction.

Unit 16	A	Front Covers
	B	Back Covers

Objective 19 Front and back covers.

Contents ...

Year 1 — TERM 2 continued

Unit 17 A A Trip to the Zoo Park
B A Trip to the Zoo Park
Objective 20 Dictionaries and alphabetical organisation.

Year 1 — TERM 3

Unit 18 A Pink Pig Turns Brown (1)
B Pink Pig Turns Brown (1)
Objective 7   Using titles, cover pages and 'blurbs'.

Unit 19 A Pink Pig Turns Brown (2)
B Pink Pig Turns Brown (2)
Objective 5   Main points and significant incidents in stories.

Unit 20 A Pink Pig Turns Brown (3)
B Pink Pig Turns Brown (3)
Objective 5   Main points and significant incidents in stories.

Unit 21 A Blue Paint
B Blue Paint
Objective 5   Main points and significant incidents in stories.

Unit 22 A When Sam goes to School
B Getting Ready for School
Objective 18 Sequence of events.

Unit 23 A Matching Labels
B Matching Labels
Objective 19 Questions and answers.

Unit 24 A Fish (Labelled Diagrams)
B Parrots (Labelled Diagrams)
Objective 19 Questions and answers.

Year 2 — TERM 1

Unit 1 A Ben's Invitation
B Ben's Invitation
Objective 14 Key Structural Features.

Unit 2 A Joe and his Grandad (1)
B Joe and his Grandad (2)
Objective 4   Time and sequential relationships in stories.

Unit 3 A Joe and his Grandad (3)
B Joe and his Grandad (4)
Objective 4   Time and sequential relationships in stories.

Unit 4 A Abbie's Parcel
B Abbie's Parcel
Objective 4   Time and sequential relationships in stories.

Unit 5 A Using the Computer
B Using the Computer
Objective 4   Time and sequential relationships in stories.

Unit 6 A Kim's Holiday Journey
B Kim's Holiday Journey
Objective 5   Reasons for events in stories.

Unit 7 A Sally and the Robin (Part1)
B Sally and the Robin (Part2)
Objective 5   Reasons for events in stories.

Unit 8 A Tom and Tim's Mishap
B Tom and Tim's Mishap
Objective 7   Learn, reread and recite favourite poems.

© Andrew Brodie Publications ✓ www.acblack.com

Contents ...

Year 2   TERM 1 continued

- **Unit 9**   A   Department Stores
  - B   Department Stores
  - Objective 14   Key Structural Features.
- **Unit 10**   A   Making a Model Tepee
  - B   Making a Model Tepee
  - Objective 13 Simple Written Instructions.
- **Unit 11**   A   Crossing the Road Safely
  - B   Crossing the Road Safely
  - Objective 14 Key structural features.

Year 2   TERM 2

- **Unit 12**   A   Jamie's Puppy
  - B   Jamie's Puppy
  - Objective 4   To predict story endings/incidents.
- **Unit 13**   A   Young Frog Part 1
  - B   Young Frog Part 1
  - Objective 4   To predict story endings/incidents.
- **Unit 14**   A   Young Frog Part 2
  - B   Young Frog Part 2
  - Objective 4   To predict story endings/incidents.
- **Unit 15**   A   The Two Jays
  - B   The Two Jays
  - Objective 6   Identify and describe characters.
- **Unit 16**   A   Toad Poem
  - B   Toad Poem
  - Objective 9   Patterns of rhythm and rhyme.
- **Unit 17**   A   What David Saw
  - B   What David Saw
  - Objective 9   Patterns of rhythm and rhyme.
- **Unit 18**   A   Dressing Up
  - B   Dressing Up
  - Objective 9   Patterns of rhythm and rhyme.
- **Unit 19**   A   The Glossary
  - B   The Glossary
  - Objective 16 Dictionaries and glossaries.

Year 2   TERM 3

- **Unit 20**   A   The Owl and the Pussy-Cat
  - B   The Owl and the Pussy-Cat
  - Objective 6   Humorous stories, extracts and poems.
- **Unit 21**   A   The Owl and the Pussy-Cat
  - B   The Owl and the Pussy-Cat
  - Objective 6   Humorous stories, extracts and poems.
- **Unit 22**   A   Caring for Your Dog
  - B   Caring for Your Dog
  - Objective 15 Contents and index.
- **Unit 23**   A   Teachers' Page - High Frequency Words
  - B   Teachers' Assessment Page - High Frequency Words
  - C   Jill's Bad Day
  - D   Jill's Bad Day
  - E   Jill's Bad Day (Questions)
  - F   Alphabetical Order
  - Key Objective   Assessment and recognition of high frequency words.

This unit addresses the Literacy Strategy:
Term 1, 2, 3   objective   1:   to reinforce and apply their word-level skills through shared and guided reading.
Term 1, 2, 3   objective   2:   to use phonological, contextual, grammatical and graphic knowledge to work out, predict, and check the meanings of unfamiliar words and to make sense of what they read.

YEAR 1 | UNIT 1 | Sheet A   Name _____   The Castle

The Castle

The children in Class 1 had some lovely toys in the classroom. There were games, puzzles, bricks, dolls and cars. In the corner of the room was a play house, which sometimes turned into a hospital, a post office or a cafe.

Miss Brown the teacher let the children choose what to play with when their work was finished.

Draw a ring around the correct answers.

☐ Which two of the toys below, were in Class 1?

        teddies   **cars**   **puzzles**

☐ The teacher was called ...

    Miss Green.   **Mr Brown.**   **Miss Brown.**

☐ What was in the corner of the room?

    a castle   **a sink**   **a play house**

☐ Which class did Miss Brown teach?

    Class 1   **Class 2**   **Class 3**

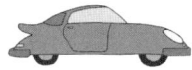  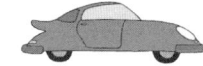  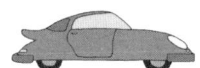

© Andrew Brodie Publications ✓ www.acblack.com

YEAR	UNIT	Sheet
1	1	B

Name   Sal and Taz (1)

Sal and Taz liked building with the bricks. There were red, blue and yellow bricks, bricks that looked like windows and bricks that looked like doors.

On Friday the two children enjoyed making a very big castle of bricks. Miss Brown said it was the best castle she had seen. Sal and Taz were very pleased.

Now answer these questions. Tick the correct answers.

Who liked playing with the bricks?
- [ ] **Sam and Tim**
- [ ] **Sal and Taz**
- [ ] **Simon and Jaz**
- [ ] **Sal and Tom**

What colour were the bricks?
- [ ] **red, blue and yellow**
- [ ] **yellow, white and red**
- [ ] **green, red, and blue**
- [ ] **black, white and pink**

What did Sal and Taz make with the bricks?
- [ ] **a house**
- [ ] **a school**
- [ ] **a castle**

Draw your favourite classroom toy.

This unit addresses the Literacy Strategy:
Term 1, 2, 3 objective   1: to reinforce and apply their word-level skills through shared and guided reading.
Term 1, 2, 3 objective   2: to use phonological, contextual, grammatical and graphic knowledge to work out, predict, and check the meanings of unfamiliar words and to make sense of what they read.
You may also find it helpful when covering :
Term 1 objective 13: to read and follow simple instructions, e.g. for classroom routines, lists for groups in workbooks.
Also Word Level Work - rhyming words.

YEAR 1 | UNIT 2 | Sheet A   Name   Rhyming Words

Rhyming Words

Choose words from the box to complete the rhymes. Colour the pictures correctly.

crown	pen
mat	dish
hair	crow

The clown with a _ _ _ _ _ wore a red and green gown.

The cat on the _ _ _ had a blue spotted hat.

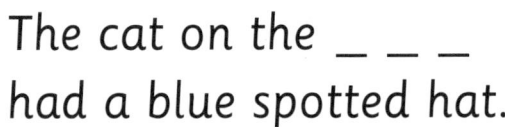

 Name   Rhyming Words

The bear with blue _ _ _ _
sat on a brown chair.

The hen with a _ _ _
drew five orange men.

I wish I had a _ _ _ _
that was full of yellow fish.

Now colour this rainbow.

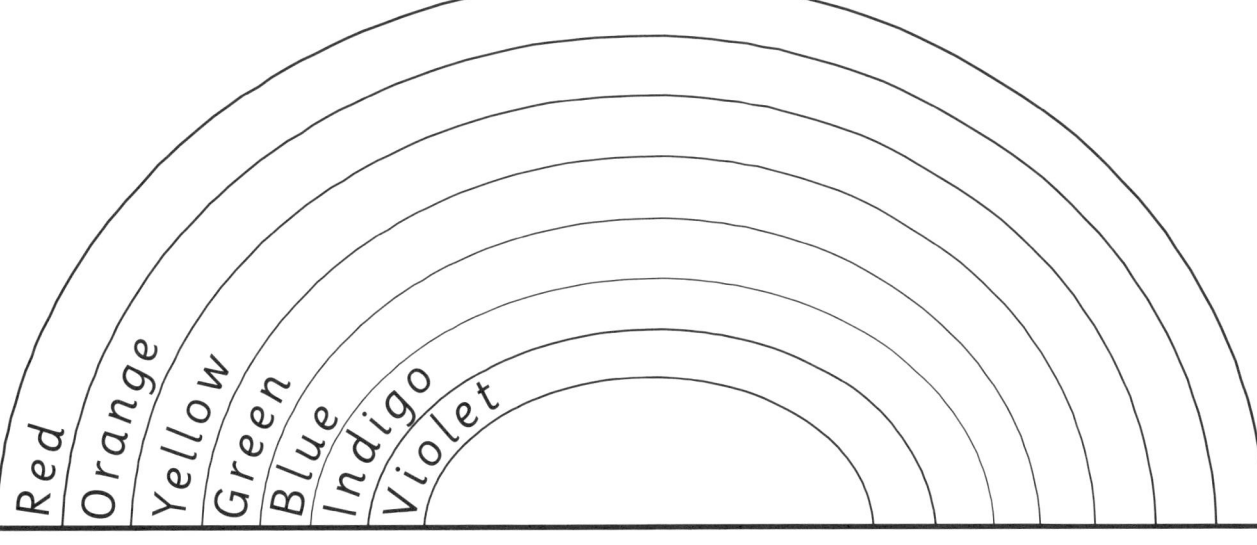

© Andrew Brodie Publications ✓ www.acblack.com

This unit addresses the Literacy Strategy:
Term 1, 2, 3 objective 1: to reinforce and apply their word-level skills through shared and guided reading.
Term 1, 2, 3 objective 2: to use phonological, contextual, grammatical and graphic knowledge to work out, predict, and check the meanings of unfamiliar words and to make sense of what they read.
You may also find it helpful when covering :
Term 1 objective 13: to read and follow simple instructions, e.g. for classroom routines, lists for groups in workbooks.

YEAR 1 | UNIT 3 | Sheet A   Name   Common Colour Words

Common Colour Words

Colour the trees **green**.

Colour the school **red**.

Colour the flowers **pink**.

Colour the house **grey**.

Colour the birds **black**.

Colour the sun **yellow**.

Colour the sky **blue**.

Colour the dog **brown**.

© Andrew Brodie Publications ✓ www.acblack.com

Days of the Week

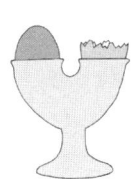
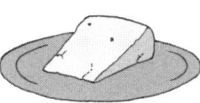

On Monday I had cheese for dinner.
On Tuesday I had eggs for tea.
On Wednesday I played in the garden.
On Thursday night I hurt my knee.
On Friday I drank a glass of milk.
On Saturday I went out to play.
On Sunday I learned to ride my bike.
It was Monday again the very next day.

Tick the correct answers.

I had eggs for tea on

☐ **Sunday**. ☐ **Monday**. ☐ **Tuesday**.

The day after Tuesday is

☐ **Wednesday**. ☐ **Thursday**. ☐ **Friday**.

Did I learn to ride my bike on Tuesday?

☐ **Yes** ☐ **No**

Did I drink milk on Friday?

☐ **Yes** ☐ **No**

What did I do on Thursday?

☐ **I hurt my knee.** ☐ **I played in the garden.**

© Andrew Brodie Publications ✓ www.acblack.com

This unit addresses the Literacy Strategy:
Term 1, 2, 3 objective 1: to reinforce and apply their word-level skills through shared and guided reading.
Term 1, 2, 3 objective 2: to use phonological, contextual, grammatical and graphic knowledge to work out, predict, and check the meanings of unfamiliar words and to make sense of what they read.

YEAR 1 | UNIT 4 | Sheet A   Name   Joey's Day Out

Joey's Day Out

The pictures about 'Joey's day Out' are not finished.

Read the writing under each one and use what you have read to finish each picture.

Joey, the dog, went for a walk. He went out of the gate and down the road to the bus stop. He had with him a bucket and spade, which he carried in his mouth.

When a number 7 bus came Joey got on! He sat by the window and looked out at the houses and gardens.

© Andrew Brodie Publications ✓ www.acblack.com

YEAR 1 | UNIT 4 | Sheet B   Name   Joey's Day Out

③

Then he saw the sea and he knew it was time to get off. He ran down to the beach carrying his bucket and spade. The sun was shining.

④

Joey put down his bucket and spade and went to play by the sea. Another dog came along and they had great fun together.

⑤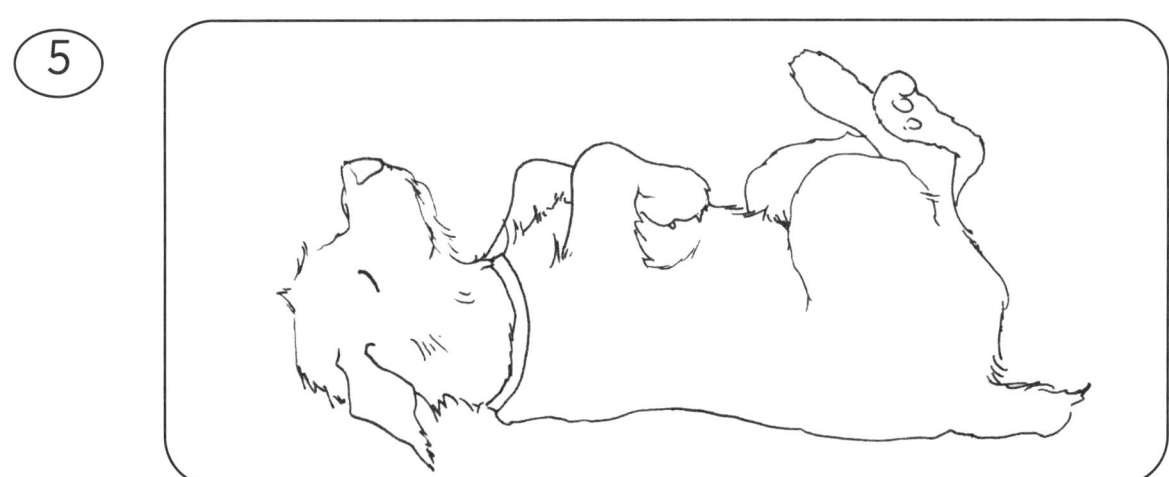

When he was tired, Joey went home again. He lay down in the garden by the flower bed and went to sleep.
Now you can colour the pictures.

The Gingerbread Man

A little old lady made a Gingerbread Man for her tea.

The Gingerbread Man then ran away saying, "Run, run, as fast as you can. You can't catch me I'm the Gingerbread Man."

The Gingerbread Man ran past some children who wanted him for their tea.
The Gingerbread Man ran away saying, "Run, run, as fast as you can. You can't catch me I'm the Gingerbread Man."

| YEAR 1 | UNIT 5 | Sheet B | Name | The Gingerbread Man |

The Gingerbread Man ran past a farmer who wanted him for his tea.
The Gingerbread man ran away saying,
"Run, run, as fast as you can. You can't catch me I'm the Gingerbread Man."

The Gingerbread Man ran past a fox.
The fox caught him and ate him for his tea!

Draw a Gingerbread Man

The Walk

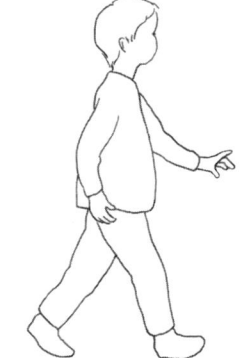 I went for a walk.
My dog came too.

 We met a cat.
The cat came too.

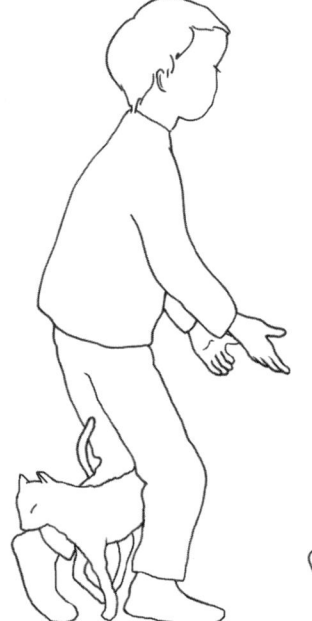 We met a rabbit.
The rabbit came too.

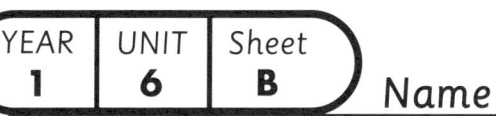

Name — The Walk

We met a mouse.
The mouse came too.

We met a bird.

The bird just flew.

Copy the words:

dog   cat   rabbit   mouse   bird

© Andrew Brodie Publications ✓ www.acblack.com

This unit addresses the Literacy Strategy:
Term 1, 2, 3 objective 1: to reinforce and apply their word-level skills through shared and guided reading.
Term 1, 2, 3 objective 2: to use phonological, contextual, grammatical and graphic knowledge to work out, predict, and check the meanings of unfamiliar words and to make sense of what they read.
You may also find it helpful when covering :
Term 1 objective 12: to read and use captions, e.g. labels around the school, on equipment.

YEAR 1 | UNIT 7 | Sheet A

Name _____   Labels and Captions

The Classroom

Write the correct word
in each label.

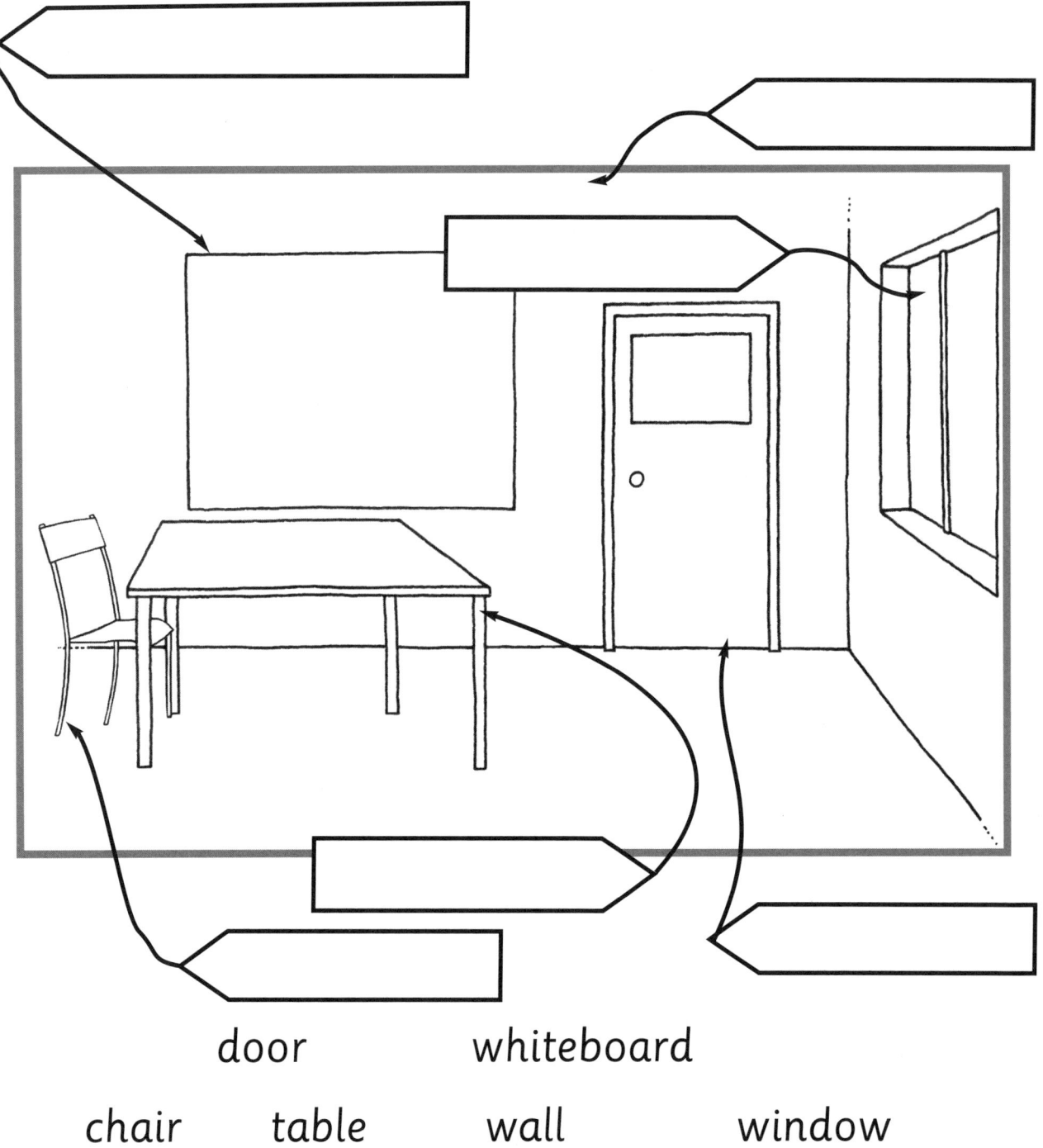

door   whiteboard

chair   table   wall   window

Now colour the picture.

© Andrew Brodie Publications ✓ www.acblack.com

| YEAR 1 | UNIT 7 | Sheet B |

Name   Labels and Captions

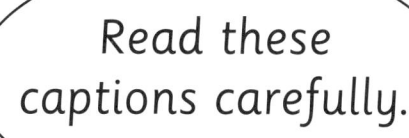 Read these captions carefully.

- A classroom with pictures on the wall.
- Lots of children in the playground.
- A house in a busy street.
- Cars, lorries and vans on a road.

Write the correct caption under the picture.

Now colour the picture.

On the back, draw and colour another picture to match one of the captions.

© Andrew Brodie Publications ✓ www.acblack.com

This unit addresses the Literacy Strategy:
Term 1, 2, 3 objective   2: to use phonological, contextual, grammatical and graphic knowledge to work out, predict, and check the meanings of unfamiliar words and to make sense of what they read.
Term 1 objective 12: to read and use captions ....
Term 1 objective 13: to read and follow simple instructions, e.g. for classroom routines, lists for groups in workbooks.

| YEAR 1 | UNIT 8 | Sheet A |

Name

Labelling Pictures

Match the labels to the picture.

We have done one for you.

chimney

roof

window

window

door

window

window

Write the words.

Now colour the house.

© Andrew Brodie Publications ✓ www.acblack.com

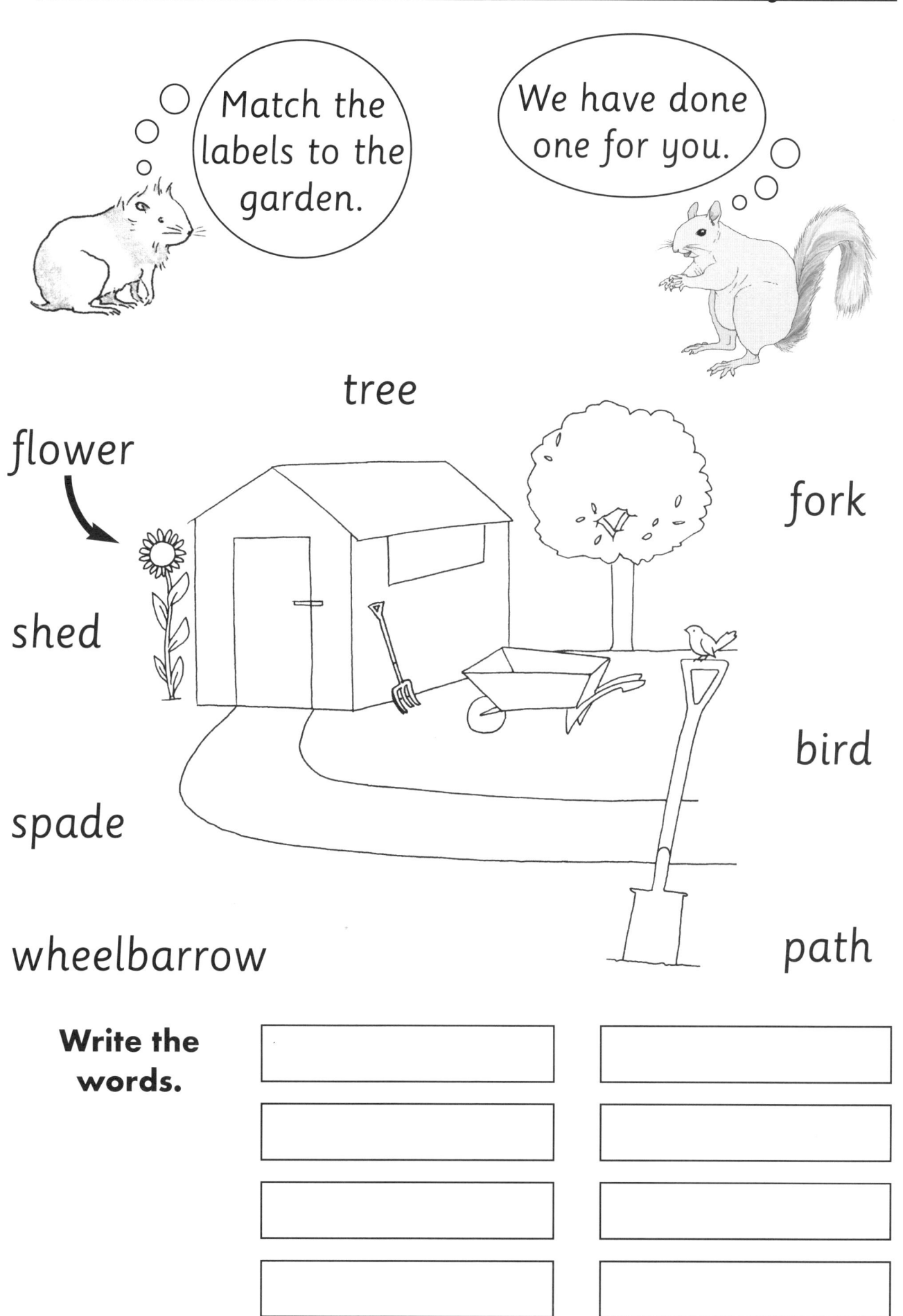

Now colour the garden.

This unit addresses the Literacy Strategy:
Term 1, 2, 3 objective   1: to reinforce and apply their word-level skills through shared and guided reading.
Term 1, 2, 3 objective   2: to use phonological, contextual, grammatical and graphic knowledge to work out, predict, and check the meanings of unfamiliar words and to make sense of what they read.
You may also find it helpful when covering :
Term 1 objective 13: to read and follow simple instructions, e.g. for classroom routines, lists for groups in workbooks.

YEAR	UNIT	Sheet
1	9	A

Name   The House

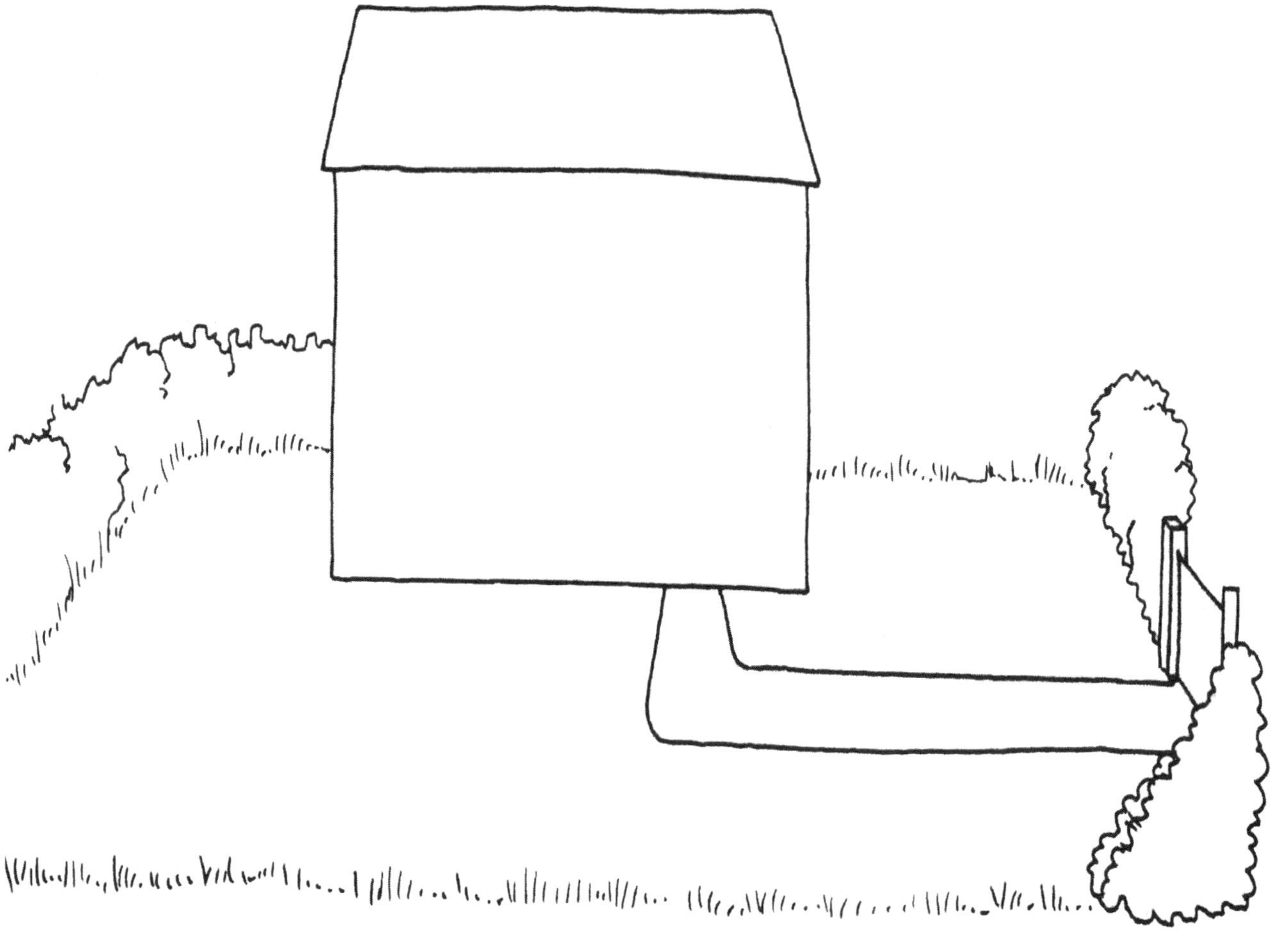

The House

1. Draw a door for the house. Colour the door red.

2. Draw four windows on the house.

3. Draw curtains in the windows. Colour them blue.

4. Colour the walls orange.

5. Colour the roof yellow.

6. Draw a tree in the garden.

7. Colour the grass green.

© Andrew Brodie Publications ✓ www.acblack.com

| YEAR 1 | UNIT 9 | Sheet B | Name | The House |

Draw a picture of a house. Write labels on your picture.

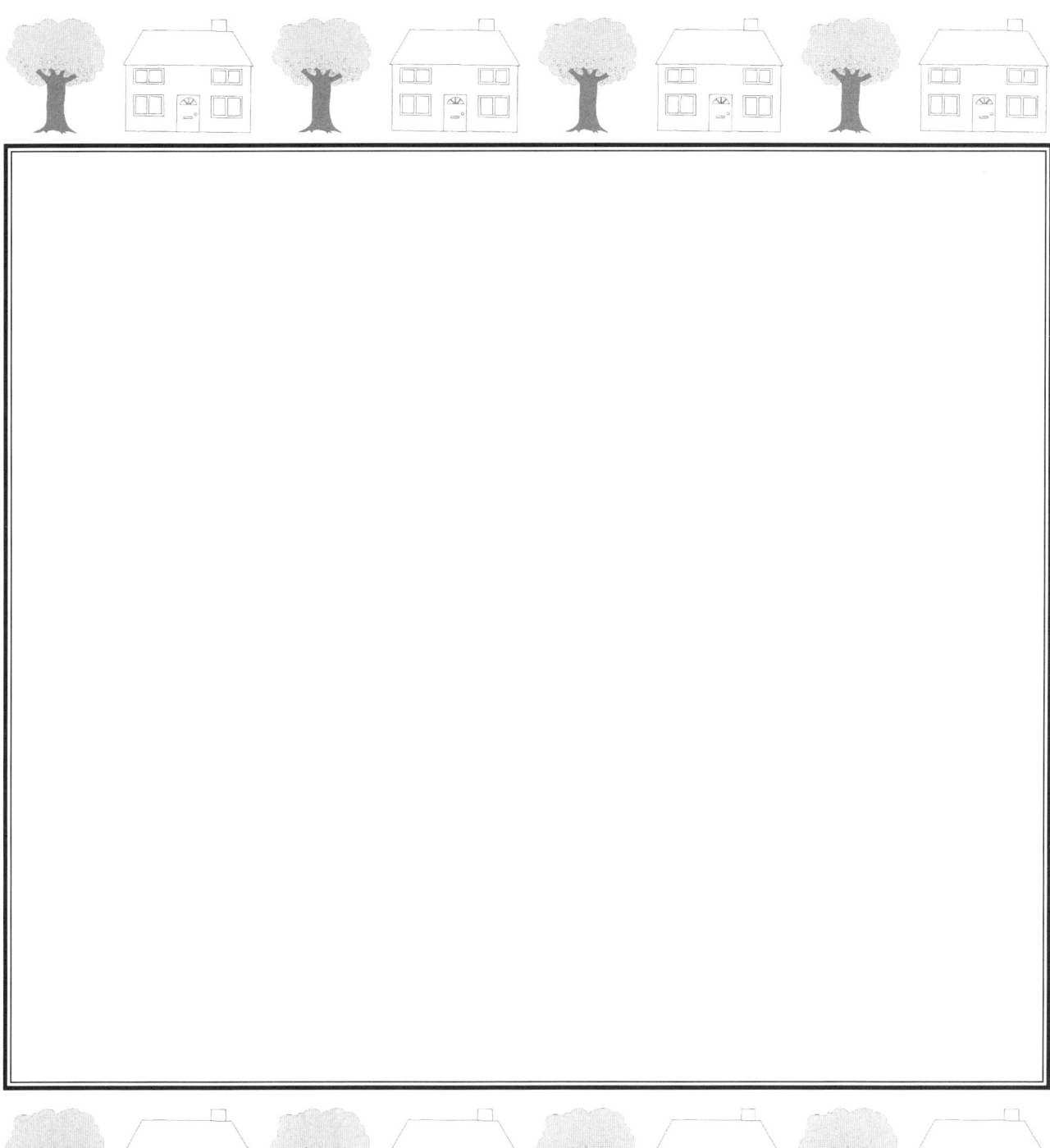

Here are some words that you might need:

tree window chimney

door roof

This unit addresses the Literacy Strategy:
Term 1, 2, 3 objective   1:   to reinforce and apply their word-level skills through shared and guided reading.
Term 1, 2, 3 objective   2:   to use phonological, contextual, grammatical and graphic knowledge to work out, predict, and check the meanings of unfamiliar words and to make sense of what they read.
You may also find it helpful when covering :
Term 2 objective   4:   to retell stories, giving the main points in sequence and to notice differences between written and spoken forms in retelling, e.g. by comparing oral versions with the written text; to refer to relevant phrases and sentences.
Term 1   objective   6:   to recite stories and rhymes with predictable and repeated patterns, extemporising on patterns orally by substituting words and phrases, extending patterns and playing with rhyme.

YEAR 1	UNIT 10	Sheet A

Name   My Day

My Day

Match the pictures to the sentences.

I went to school at 9 o'clock.

I woke up at 7 o'clock.

I had lunch at 1 o'clock.

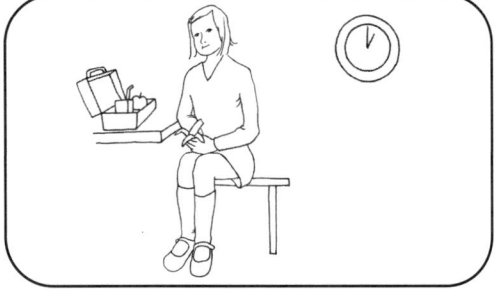

I got dressed at 8 o'clock.

© Andrew Brodie Publications ✓ www.acblack.com

This unit addresses the Literacy Strategy:
Term 1, 2, 3 objective   1: to reinforce and apply their word-level skills through shared and guided reading.
Term 1, 2, 3 objective   2: to use phonological, contextual, grammatical and graphic knowledge to work out, predict, and check the meanings of unfamiliar words and to make sense of what they read.
You may also find it helpful when covering :
Term 2 objective   7: to discuss reasons for, or causes of, incidents in stories.

| YEAR 1 | UNIT 11 | Sheet A |

Name _____   Taz and Sal Story (2)

This story doesn't have a title.

Read it with care.

Title _____

It was a sunny day in the summer holidays, and Sal and Taz went out for the day. They went to the park with Dad. All three of them enjoyed playing ball before having a picnic.

At one o'clock the picnic was spread out and the food put out ready for the children to eat. Sal ate egg sandwiches and cheese and onion crisps. Taz munched cheese sandwiches and salt and vinegar crisps. Both children had chocolate buns, apples and a drink of orange squash.

Tick the correct answer.

○ Who took the children to the park?
  ☐ **Mum**   ☐ **Dad**   ☐ **Grandad**

○ What did they do before lunch?
  ☐ **played on the swings**   ☐ **played ball**

○ What sort of sandwiches did Sal have?
  ☐ **egg**   ☐ **cheese**   ☐ **meat**

○ What flavour crisps did Taz eat?
  ☐ **salt and vinegar**   ☐ **cheese and onion**

On the top line, write a good title for the story.

© Andrew Brodie Publications ✓ www.acblack.com

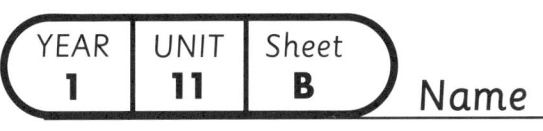 Name   Taz and Sal Story (2)

Here is the rest of the story.

After the meal Sal and Taz went down to the pond and fed the ducks. Later they played on the swings, slides and roundabouts.

At six o'clock Dad said it was time to go home. The children were sad to leave the park, but they were both very tired after their lovely day out.

Write the answers to these questions.

○ What sort of fruit did the children eat?
_____

○ Who said it was time to go home?
_____

○ What did the children do at the pond?
_____

○ Why do you think the children felt sad when they had to leave the park? _____
_____

In the box draw a picture of yourself having a picnic. Label the foods you would choose on your picnic. Colour your picture.

This unit addresses the Literacy Strategy:
Term 1, 2, 3 objective   1: to reinforce and apply their word-level skills through shared and guided reading.
Term 1, 2, 3 objective   2: to use phonological, contextual, grammatical and graphic knowledge to work out, predict, and check the meanings of unfamiliar words and to make sense of what they read.
You may also find it helpful when covering :
Term 2 objective   8: to identify and discuss characters, e.g. appearance, behaviour, qualities; to speculate about how they might behave; to discuss how they are described in the text and to compare characters from different stories or plays.

YEAR 1 | UNIT 12 | Sheet A   Name   Finish the Picture

Finish the Picture

Read the sentences, then finish the picture.

The man has a beard.

He is wearing glasses.

He has black hair.

His tie is blue.

His jacket is brown and his trousers are green.

He has brown shoes.

Don't forget to draw the man's eyes and his mouth and his nose.

© Andrew Brodie Publications ✓ www.acblack.com

| YEAR 1 | UNIT 12 | Sheet B | Name | Finish the Picture |

Read the sentences, then finish the picture.

The old lady is sitting in a big chair.

She has a blue dress.

The chair is red with pink flowers.

The dog is brown.

Now draw a picture of a man with a cat.
Write some sentences about your picture.

© Andrew Brodie Publications ✓ www.acblack.com

This unit addresses the Literacy Strategy:
Term 1, 2, 3 objective   1: to reinforce and apply their word-level skills through shared and guided reading.
Term 1, 2, 3 objective   2: to use phonological, contextual, grammatical and graphic knowledge to work out, predict, and check the meanings of unfamiliar words and to make sense of what they read.
You may also find it helpful when covering :
Term 1 objective   4: to read familiar, simple stories and poems independently, to point while reading and make correspondence between words said and read.
Term 2 objective   8: to identify and discuss characters, e.g. appearance, behaviour, qualities; to speculate about how they might behave; to discuss how they are described in the text; and to compare characters from different stories or plays.

YEAR 1 | UNIT 13 | Sheet A   Name   Humpty Dumpty

Humpty Dumpty

Humpty Dumpty sat on a wall.
Humpty Dumpty had a great fall.
All the king's horses.
And all the king's men.
Couldn't put Humpty together again.

Draw a ring around the correct answer.

What did Humpty Dumpty sit on?

        a wall   **a chair**   **the grass**

What happened to Humpty Dumpty?

        He danced.   **He fell.**   **He walked.**

What were the king's men riding on?

        bikes   **donkeys**   **horses**

Did they put Humpty Dumpty together again?

        yes   **no**

Now you may colour the pictures.

© Andrew Brodie Publications ✓ www.acblack.com

Jack and Jill

Jack and Jill went up the hill,
To fetch a pail of water.
Jack fell down and broke his crown,
And Jill came tumbling after.

Tick the correct answers.

Who were in the rhyme?

☐ **Jack and John** ☐ **John and Joan**

☐ **Jack and Jenny** ☐ **Jack and Jill**

Where were they going?

☐ **down a hill** ☐ **up a hill**

What were they going for?

☐ **water** ☐ **orange juice** ☐ **bananas**

What do you think a crown is?

☐ **arm** ☐ **leg**

☐ **neck** ☐ **head**

How did Jill go down the hill?

☐ **She tumbled.**

☐ **She ran.**

Now you can colour the picture.

© Andrew Brodie Publications ✓ www.acblack.com

This unit addresses the Literacy Strategy:
Term 1, 2, 3 objective 1: to reinforce and apply their word-level skills through shared and guided reading.
Term 1, 2, 3 objective 2: to use phonological, contextual, grammatical and graphic knowledge to work out, predict, and check the meanings of unfamiliar words and to make sense of what they read.
You may also find it helpful when covering :
Term 2 objective 11: to learn and recite poems and rhymes, with actions, and to reread them from the text.

Name

Nursery Rhymes

Do you know these rhymes?
Point to each word as you say them.

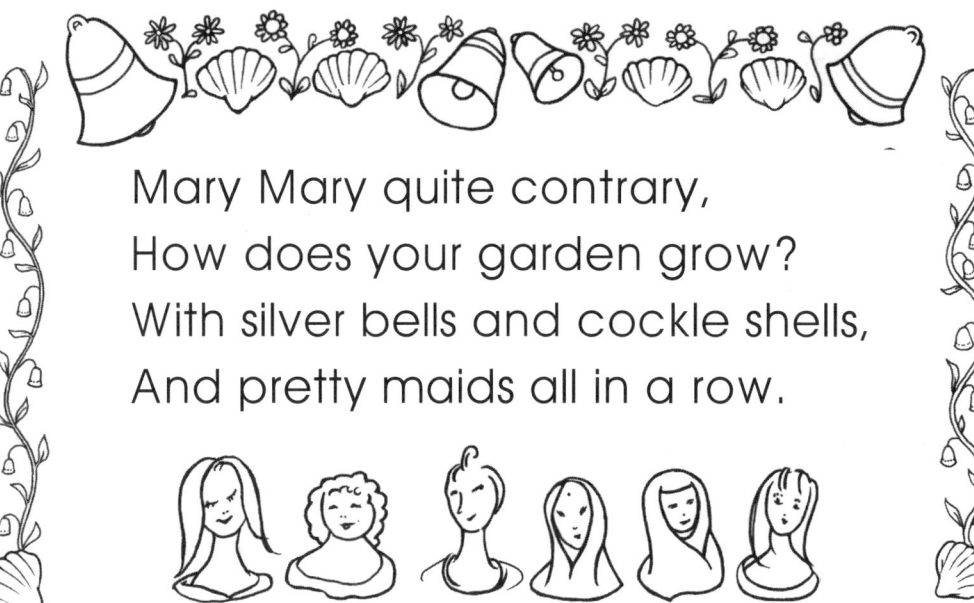

Mary Mary quite contrary,
How does your garden grow?
With silver bells and cockle shells,
And pretty maids all in a row.

Hickory Dickory Dock,

The mouse ran up the clock.

The clock struck ONE,

The mouse ran down.

Hickory Dickory Dock.

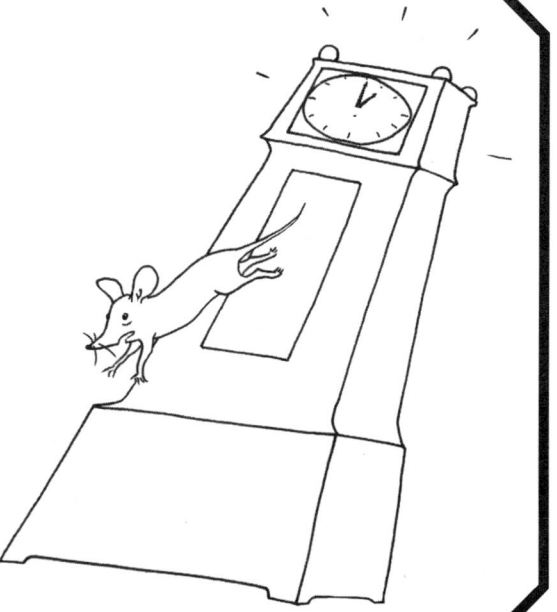

| YEAR 1 | UNIT 14 | Sheet B | Name | Action Rhymes |

Make up some actions to do with this rhyme.

Five little teddy bears all in a row,
One said, "It's time for school,
I'll have to go."

Four little teddy bears all in a row,
One said, "It's time for play,
I'll have to go."

Three little teddy bears all in a row,
One said, "It's time for tea,
I'll have to go."

Two little teddy bears all in a row,
One said, "It's time for a bath,
I'll have to go."

One little teddy bear all on his own,
He said, "It's time for bed,
Moan, moan, moan!"

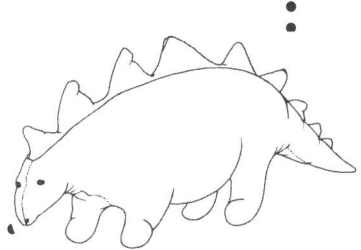

5 little bears in a row...

© Andrew Brodie Publications ✓ www.acblack.com

This unit addresses the Literacy Strategy:
Term 1, 2, 3 objective   1: to reinforce and apply their word-level skills through shared and guided reading.
Term 1, 2, 3 objective   2: to use phonological, contextual, grammatical and graphic knowledge to work out, predict, and check the meanings of unfamiliar words and to make sense of what they read.
You may also find it helpful when covering :
Term 2 objective 17: to use terms 'fiction' and 'non-fiction', noting some of their differing features, e.g. layout, titles, contents page, use of pictures, labelled diagrams.

YEAR	UNIT	Sheet
1	15	A

Name

A Bear Tale (Fiction)

A Bear Tale

One day a little girl went for a walk in the woods. She watched the birds flying in the sky, and she picked some pretty flowers. She was very surprised when she met a very large brown bear.

"I am rather hungry," said the bear.

"Would you like some of my chocolate?" asked the girl.

"No thank-you," said the bear, "I would rather eat you."

So he did.

Tick the correct answers.

✳ What did the girl watch?

☐ **cows**   ☐ **birds**   ☐ **flowers**   ☐ **sheep**

✳ What did the bear say?   ☐ **"How nice to meet you."**

☐ **"I am ready for dinner."**

☐ **"I would like some chocolate."**

☐ **"I am rather hungry."**

© Andrew Brodie Publications ✓ www.acblack.com

Now read this information about bears.

Bears

Bears are furry animals with four legs. They have sharp claws and can be very dangerous.

Polar bears have white fur and live in the Arctic where it is very cold.

Two other sorts of bear are the brown bear and the grizzly bear.

Wild bears can be found in many parts of the world, but not in Britain.

✷ What is the title of the text?

_____

✷ Is the text fiction or non-fiction?

_____

✷ What colour is the fur of polar bears?

_____

✷ Are wild bears found in Britain?

_____

© Andrew Brodie Publications ✓ www.acblack.com

This unit addresses the Literacy Strategy:
Term 1, 2, 3 objective   1: to reinforce and apply their word-level skills through shared and guided reading.
Term 1, 2, 3 objective   2: to use phonological, contextual, grammatical and graphic knowledge to work out, predict, and check the meanings of unfamiliar words and to make sense of what they read.
You may also find it helpful when covering :
Term 2 objective 19: to predict what a given book might be about from a brief look at both front and back covers, including blurb, title, illustration; to discuss what it might tell in advance of reading and check to see if it does.

YEAR 1 | UNIT 16 | Sheet A   Name   Front Covers

Front and Back Covers

Write the answers to these questions.

What is the title of the book?

_____

Who is the author?

_____

Do you think it is a story book?

_____

Do you think it is an information book?

_____

What is on the picture on the front cover?

_____

© Andrew Brodie Publications ✓ www.acblack.com

| YEAR 1 | UNIT 16 | Sheet B |

Name

Back Covers

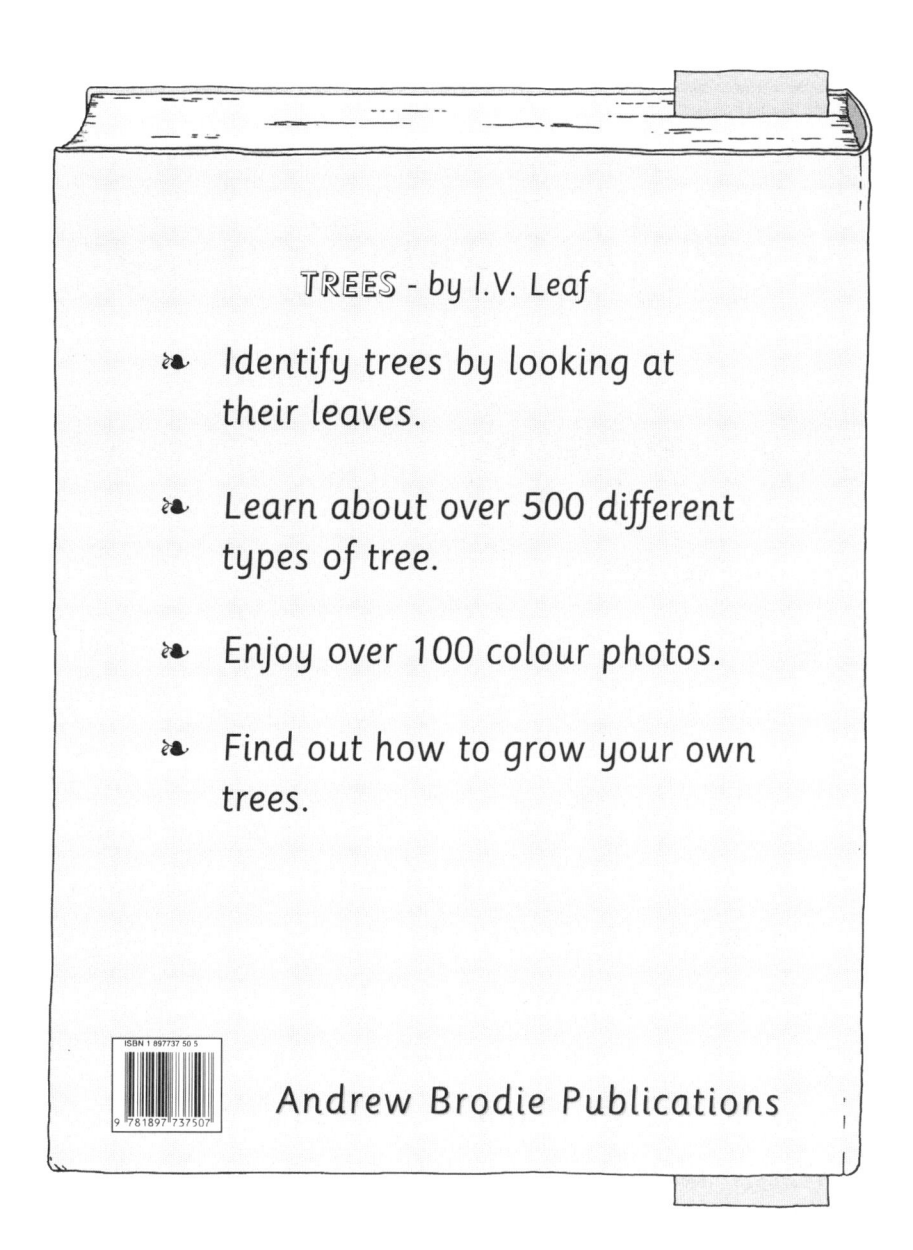

> TREES - by I.V. Leaf
>
> - Identify trees by looking at their leaves.
>
> - Learn about over 500 different types of tree.
>
> - Enjoy over 100 colour photos.
>
> - Find out how to grow your own trees.
>
> ISBN 1 897737 50 5
>
> Andrew Brodie Publications

Name the publisher of the book.

_____

How many types of tree can you find out about in the book?

_____

How many colour photographs are in the book?

_____

Now look at a book in your classroom or in the library. Look at the back of the book. What can you see?

© Andrew Brodie Publications ✓ www.acblack.com

This unit addresses the Literacy Strategy:
Term 1, 2, 3 objective   1: to reinforce and apply their word-level skills through shared and guided reading.
Term 1, 2, 3 objective   2: to use phonological, contextual, grammatical and graphic knowledge to work out, predict, and check the meanings of unfamiliar words and to make sense of what they read.
You may also find it helpful when covering :
Term 2 objective 20: to use simple dictionaries, and to understand their alphabetical organisation.

YEAR	UNIT	Sheet
1	17	A

Name _____

A Trip to the Zoo Park

A Trip to the Zoo Park
by Tani   age 6

On Saturday I went to the zoo park with my family. There were three grown-ups and four children altogether.

We went in Uncle Tom's big car with seven seats.

First we went to see the monkeys. They played with tyres.

Next we went to the penguin pool. We saw them dive into the water and then we saw them under the water through a special window in the side of the pool.

When it was lunch time we had a picnic. We could see zebras and giraffes from where we were sitting. Mum said it was like being in Africa.

© Andrew Brodie Publications ✓ www.acblack.com

| YEAR 1 | UNIT 17 | Sheet B | Name | A Trip to the Zoo Park |

Use Tani's story about a trip to the zoo park to help you fill in the missing words.
The first letter is there to help you.

Tani's family went to the zoo park on S _ _ _ _ _ _ _ _ .

First they saw some m _ _ _ _ _ _ _ .

Next they saw some p _ _ _ _ _ _ _ _ .

At lunch time they watched z _ _ _ _ _ _

and g _ _ _ _ _ _ _ _ .

Alphabetical Order

a b c d e f g h i j k l m n o p q r s t u v w x y z

Put these words in alphabetical order. Look at the letter that the word begins with and see where it comes in the alphabet. A word beginning with 'd', like duck, would come before a word beginning with 'm' like mouse.

animal   penguin   giraffe

monkey   zebra

(a _ _ _ _ _)   (g _ _ _ _ _ _)   (m _ _ _ _ _)

(p _ _ _ _ _ _)   (z _ _ _ _)

© Andrew Brodie Publications ✓ www.acblack.com

This unit addresses the Literacy Strategy:
Term 1, 2, 3 objective   1: to reinforce and apply their word-level skills through shared and guided reading.
Term 1, 2, 3 objective   2: to use phonological, contextual, grammatical and graphic knowledge to work out, predict, and check the meanings of unfamiliar words and to make sense of what they read.
You may also find it helpful when covering :
Term 3 objective   7: to use titles, cover pages, pictures and 'blurbs' to predict the content of unfamiliar stories.

YEAR 1 | UNIT 18 | Sheet A   Name   Pink Pig turns brown (1)

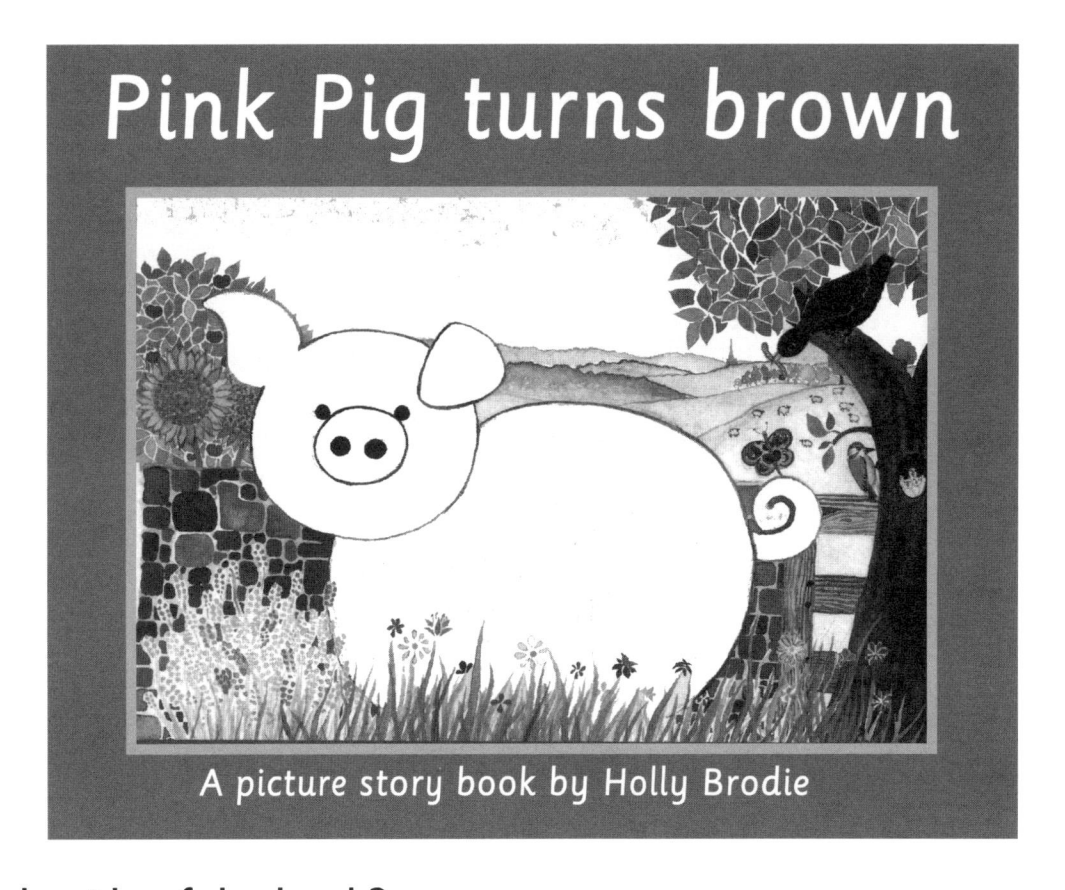

Pink Pig turns brown

A picture story book by Holly Brodie

What is the title of the book?

What animal is the book about?

Who is the author?

On the back cover of the book it says:

'Pink Pig turns brown' is the story of a little pig who wants to win a prize at the village show.

This is called the 'blurb' and it tells us about the story.

© Andrew Brodie Publications ✓ www.acblack.com

| YEAR 1 | UNIT 18 | Sheet B |

Name _____   Pink Pig turns brown (1)

Make up your own cover for a book.

1. Give it a title, for example:
    "Baby Duck's day out"
    "Daniel Dinosaur got lost"
    "Teddy at the seaside"
    "The Dragon who tried to be good"

2. Draw a picture for the cover that shows what the story is about.

3. Put your name as the author.

Title _____

A book by _____

© Andrew Brodie Publications ✓ www.acblack.com

This unit addresses the Literacy Strategy:
Term 1, 2, 3 objective   1: to reinforce and apply their word-level skills through shared and guided reading.
Term 1, 2, 3 objective   2: to use phonological, contextual, grammatical and graphic knowledge to work out, predict, and check the meanings of unfamiliar words and to make sense of what they read.
You may also find it helpful when covering :
Term 3 objective   5: to retell stories, to give the main points in sequence and to pick out significant incidents.

YEAR 1 | UNIT 19 | Sheet A   Name   Pink Pig turns brown (2)

Pink Pig turns brown

Here is the end of a story called 'Pink Pig turns brown'.

Pink Pig belongs to Farmer Plum and he is going to enter a competition in the Village Show.

Mrs Plum has just given him a bath in a tub.

He jumps out and trots back to his friends.

His friends are all playing in the mud.
They think he looks funny, all clean and pink.
Pink Pig wants to play too, but Mrs Plum will be cross if he gets dirty again.
Naughty Pig throws some mud at Pink Pig.
Oh, dear, he's sure to be in trouble now!
Soon everyone joins in the fun.

© Andrew Brodie Publications ✓ www.acblack.com

Pink Pig turns brown (2)

Pink Pig is covered in mud from ear to trotter.
Pink Pig will not win the show looking like that!
He's not pink anymore, he's brown all over.

Farmer Plum is a nice man.
"Never mind," he says.
"You will just have to be a brown pig instead of a pink pig…but hurry, it's time to go."

Farmer Plum and Pink Pig walk to the show.
The sky is turning grey.
Raindrops begin to fall.
They tickle Pink Pig's snout.
The rain is washing the mud off!
Pink Pig is turning pink again!
They arrive at the show just in time.
Pink Pig is the smartest pig there.

This unit addresses the Literacy Strategy:
Term 1, 2, 3 objective   1: to reinforce and apply their word-level skills through shared and guided reading.
Term 1, 2, 3 objective   2: to use phonological, contextual, grammatical and graphic knowledge to work out, predict, and check the meanings of unfamiliar words and to make sense of what they read.
Term 3 objective   5: to retell stories, to give the main points in sequence and to pick out significant incidents.

YEAR 1 | UNIT 20 | Sheet A   Name   Pink Pig turns brown (3)

Put a ring around the correct word in the box so that it tells the story of Pink Pig.

Pink Pig had a | shower / bath |. He was all clean

and | pink / brown |. The other | cows / pigs | threw

mud at Pink Pig and he became all muddy.

On the way to the Village | Show / Shop | it

began to | snow / rain | and it washed the mud off.

Pink Pig turned | blue / pink | again.

© Andrew Brodie Publications ✓ www.acblack.com

| YEAR 1 | UNIT 20 | Sheet B | Name _____ | Pink Pig turns brown (3) |

Draw a picture of Pink Pig winning a prize at the show.

© Andrew Brodie Publications ✓ www.acblack.com

This unit addresses the Literacy Strategy:
Term 1, 2, 3 objective   1: to reinforce and apply their word-level skills through shared and guided reading.
Term 1, 2, 3 objective   2: to use phonological, contextual, grammatical and graphic knowledge to work out, predict, and check the meanings of unfamiliar words and to make sense of what they read.
You may also find it helpful when covering :
Term 3 objective 5:   to retell stories, to give the main points in sequence and to pick out significant incidents.
Term 3 objective 6:   to prepare and retell stories orally, identifying and using some of the more formal features of story language.

YEAR 1 | UNIT 21 | Sheet A

Name   Blue Paint

Blue Paint

Read the story.

Mum went to the shop and bought a big can of blue paint. She brought it home to paint my bedroom walls. But we knocked the can over. So we painted the floor instead. I have a nice blue floor.

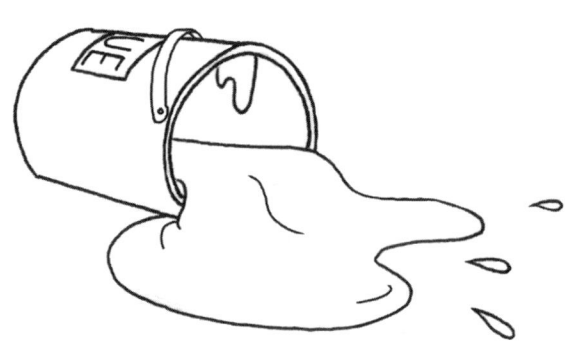

© Andrew Brodie Publications ✓ www.acblack.com

| YEAR 1 | UNIT 21 | Sheet B |

Name _____ Blue Paint

Now retell the story.

1.
2.
3.
4.
5.
6.

© Andrew Brodie Publications ✓ www.acblack.com

This unit addresses the Literacy Strategy:
Term 1, 2, 3 objective   1: to reinforce and apply their word-level skills through shared and guided reading.
Term 1, 2, 3 objective   2: to use phonological, contextual, grammatical and graphic knowledge to work out, predict, and check the meanings of unfamiliar words and to make sense of what they read.
You may also find it helpful when covering :
Term 3 objective 18: to read recounts and begin to recognise generic structure e.g. ordered sequence of events, use of words like first, next, after, when.

| YEAR 1 | UNIT 22 | Sheet A |

Name _____

When Sam goes to School

When Sam goes to School

First I get out of bed and get dressed.

Then I have breakfast.

After breakfast I clean my teeth.

Next I read my book.

When it is time to go I remember my book bag, my lunch box and my ball for play time.

© Andrew Brodie Publications ✓ www.acblack.com

| YEAR 1 | UNIT 22 | Sheet B | Name _____ | Getting Ready For School |

Draw some pictures of you getting ready for school in the morning. Make sure they are in the right order. Begin with getting up and end with leaving for school.

First I get up _____

_____

_____

Then I _____

_____

_____

Next I _____

_____

_____

Finally I leave for school and I remember to bring my _____

_____

_____

© Andrew Brodie Publications ✓ www.acblack.com

This unit addresses the Literacy Strategy:
Term 1, 2, 3 objective   1: to reinforce and apply their word-level skills through shared and guided reading.
Term 1, 2, 3 objective   2: to use phonological, contextual, grammatical and graphic knowledge to work out, predict, and check the meanings of unfamiliar words and to make sense of what they read.
You may also find it helpful when covering :
Term 3 objective 19: to identify simple questions and use text to find answers. To locate parts of text that give particular information including labelled diagrams and charts, e.g. parts of a car, what pets eat, clothes that keep us warm.

| YEAR 1 | UNIT 23 | Sheet A |

Name ....   **Matching Labels**

Match the questions to the answers. The first one has been done for you.

What is the name for a baby dog?	The last letter of the alphabet is **Z**
$2 + 3 =$	**Saturday and Sunday**
What is the last letter of the alphabet?	**5**
What are the two days that we call the weekend?	**A baby dog is called a puppy.**

© Andrew Brodie Publications ✓ www.acblack.com

| YEAR 1 | UNIT 23 | Sheet B |

Name Matching Labels

Put the labels on these pictures.

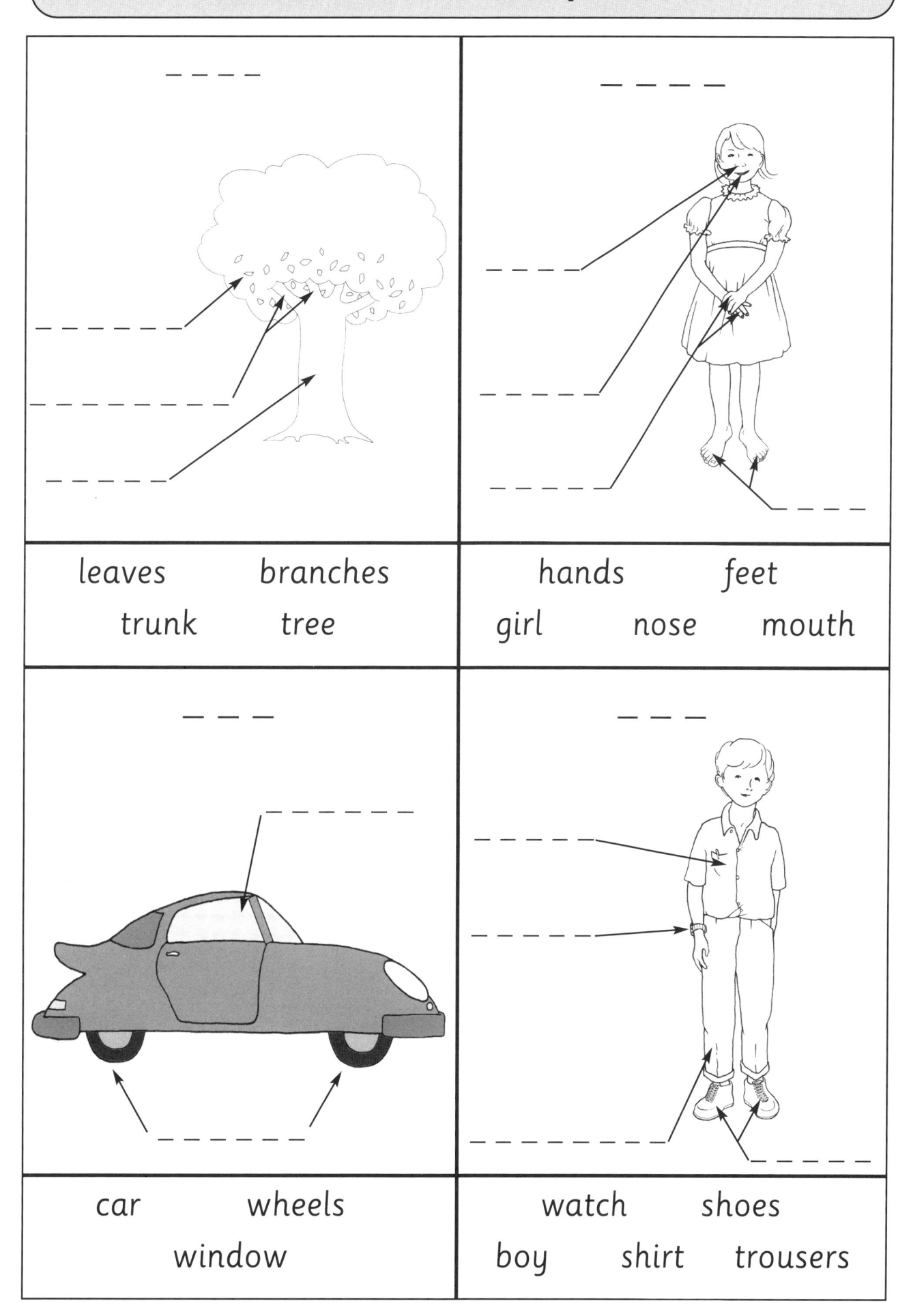

| leaves   branches trunk   tree | hands   feet girl   nose   mouth |
| car   wheels window | watch   shoes boy   shirt   trousers |

© Andrew Brodie Publications ✓ www.acblack.com

This unit addresses the Literacy Strategy:
Term 1, 2, 3 objective 1: to reinforce and apply their word-level skills through shared and guided reading.
Term 1, 2, 3 objective 2: to use phonological, contextual, grammatical and graphic knowledge to work out, predict, and check the meanings of unfamiliar words and to make sense of what they read.
You may also find it helpful when covering:
Term 3 objective 19: to identify simple questions and use text to find answers. To locate parts of text that give particular information labelled diagrams and charts. e.g. parts of a car, what pets eat, clothes that keep us warm.

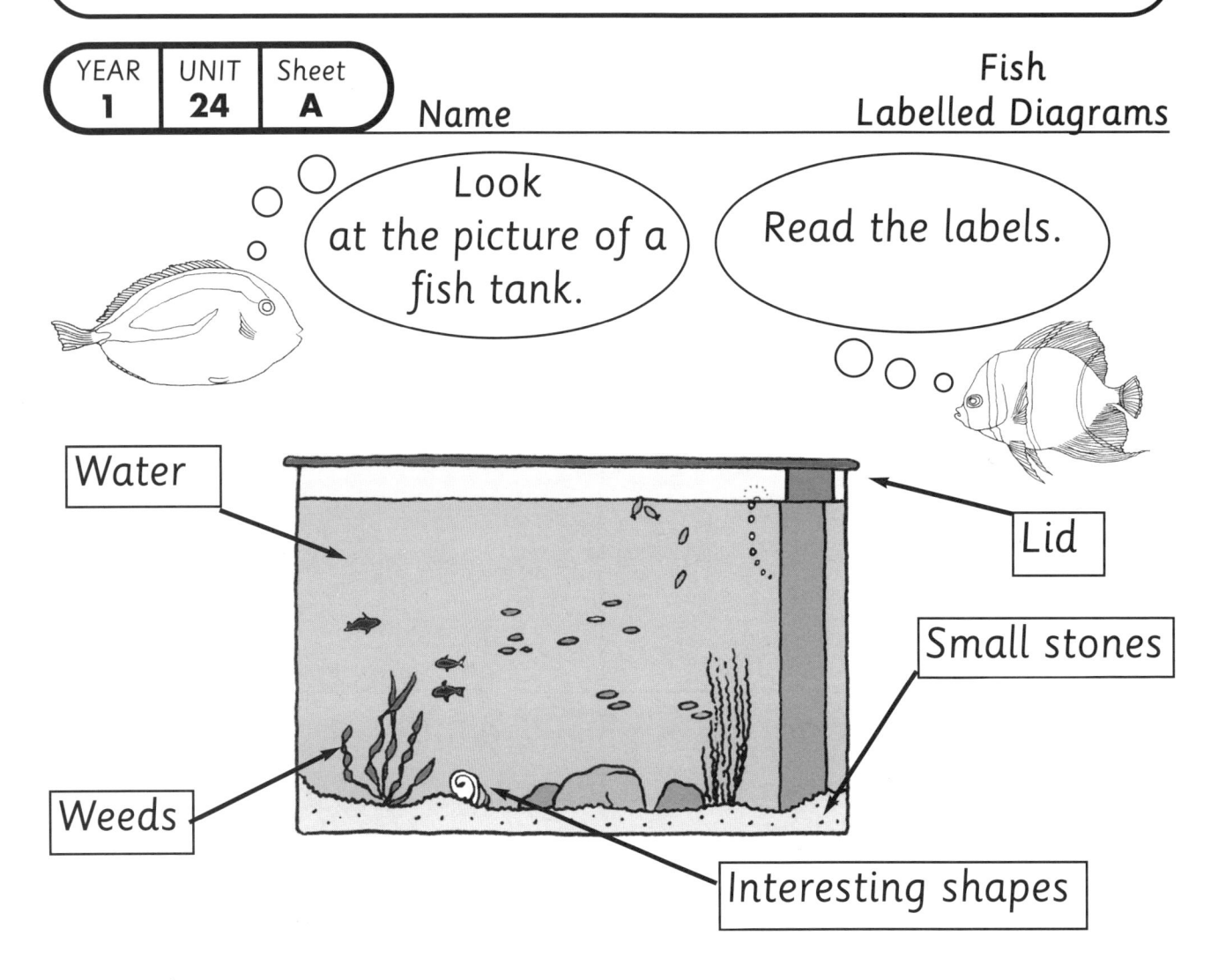

| YEAR 1 | UNIT 24 | Sheet A | Name | Fish Labelled Diagrams |

Look at the picture of a fish tank.

Read the labels.

Water

Lid

Small stones

Weeds

Interesting shapes

Ring the correct answers.

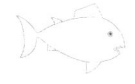

What covers the floor of the tank?

sand   earth   stones   weed

What can fish eat in the tank?

stone   weed   water   lid

Which word means the same as tank?

cage   aquarium   kennel   house

Now draw a picture of a pet you would like, and a suitable container to keep it in.

© Andrew Brodie Publications ✓ www.acblack.com

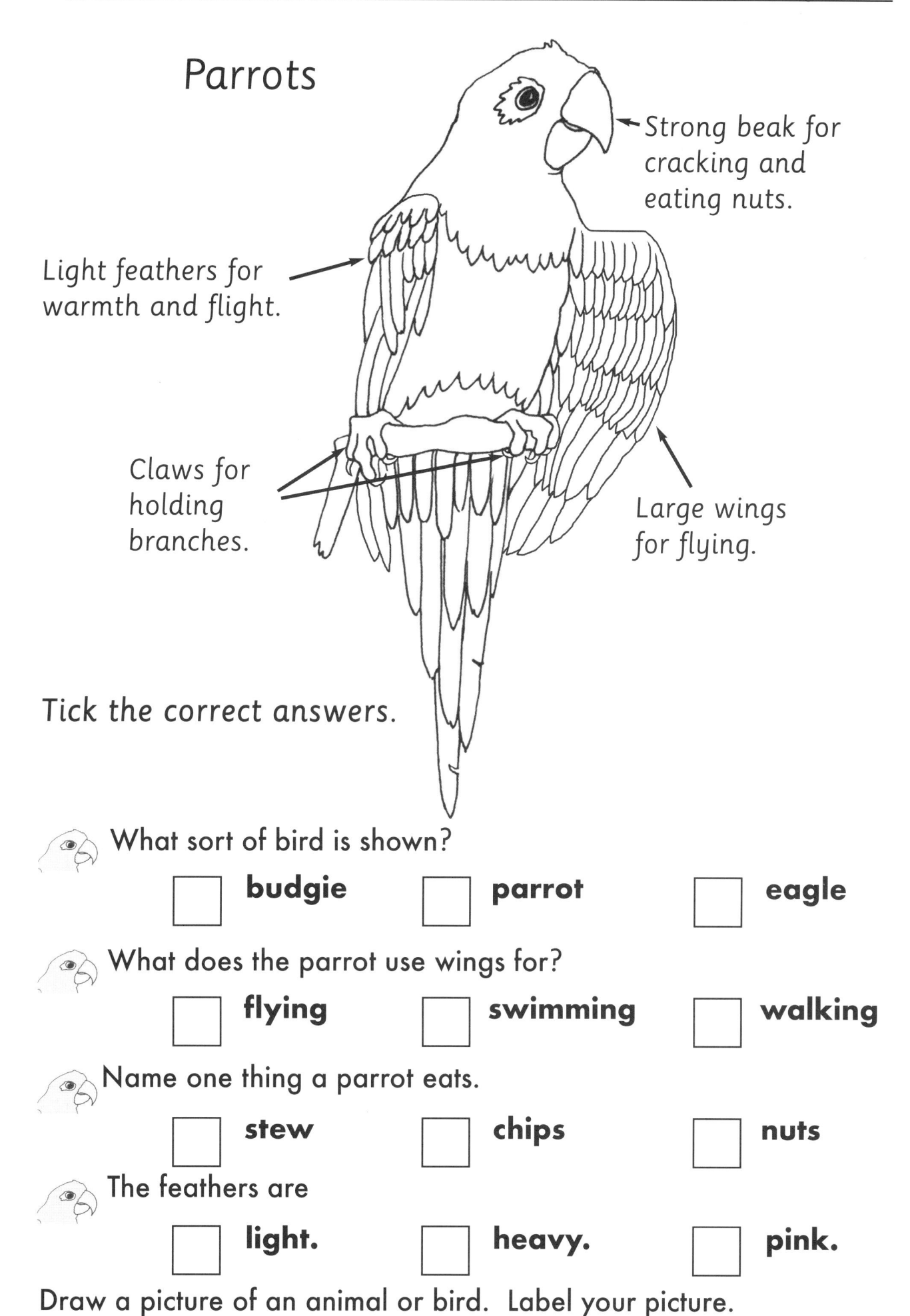

| YEAR 1 | UNIT 24 | Sheet B | Name | Parrots Labelled Diagrams |

Parrots

→ Strong beak for cracking and eating nuts.

Light feathers for warmth and flight.

Claws for holding branches.

Large wings for flying.

Tick the correct answers.

What sort of bird is shown?

☐ budgie ☐ parrot ☐ eagle

What does the parrot use wings for?

☐ flying ☐ swimming ☐ walking

Name one thing a parrot eats.

☐ stew ☐ chips ☐ nuts

The feathers are

☐ light. ☐ heavy. ☐ pink.

Draw a picture of an animal or bird. Label your picture.

© Andrew Brodie Publications ✓ www.acblack.com

This unit addresses the Literacy Strategy:
Term 1, 2, 3 objective 1: to reinforce and apply their word-level skills through shared and guided reading.
Term 1, 2, 3 objective 2: to use phonological, contextual, grammatical and graphic knowledge to work out, predict, and check the meanings of unfamiliar words and to make sense of what they read.

YEAR 2 | UNIT 1 | Sheet A

Name _____ Ben's Invitation

Ben's Invitation

Ben is seven soon. He is having a birthday party.

Here is one of the invitations he sent.

Party Invitation

To **Bella**

Ben is having a birthday party.

It is on Saturday May 29th

At Upton Village Hall

From 2 o'clock until 5 o'clock.

There will be games to play, a disco for dancing and delicious food.

Please reply to let Ben know if you will be there.

Telephone 12493 369608 or write to Ben Hall at 29 Orchard Way, Upton.

YEAR	UNIT	Sheet
2	1	B

Name   Ben's Invitation

Draw a ring around the correct answer.

✶ How old will Ben be on his birthday?

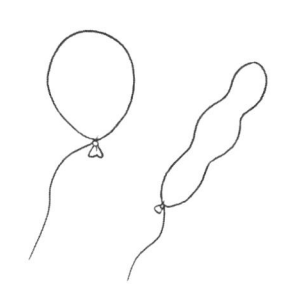

    5   **6**   **7**   **8**   **9**

✶ What day of the week is the party?

    Friday   **Saturday**   **Sunday**   **Monday**

✶ What time does the party start?

    Midday   **Five o'clock**   **Two o'clock**

✶ Who was the invitation sent to?

    Bill   **Ben**   **Belle**   **Bella**

Write the answers to these questions.

✶ Where is the party being held?

_____

_____

✶ What is the date of the party?

_____

_____

✶ What is Ben's family name?

_____

_____

✶ Name three things people might expect to do at the party.

_____

_____

**On the back of the sheet,
design a party invitation for your next birthday.**

© Andrew Brodie Publications ✓ www.acblack.com

This unit addresses the Literacy Strategy:
Term 1, 2, 3 objective   1: to reinforce and apply their word-level skills through shared and guided reading.
Term 1, 2, 3 objective   2: to use phonological, contextual, grammatical and graphic knowledge to work out, predict, and check the meanings of unfamiliar words and to make sense of what they read.
You may also find it helpful when covering :
Term 1 objective 4: to understand time and sequential relationships in stories, i.e. what happened when.

YEAR 2 | UNIT 2 | Sheet A   Name _____   Joe and his Grandad

Joe and his Grandad - Part 1

Joe liked to visit his Grandad. It was a long journey to Grandad's house, but Joe didn't mind as he always had such fun when he got there.

On the first Saturday morning of the school summer holidays, Mum and Dad took Joe to stay with Grandad for a whole week. Joe was very excited. He packed his clothes, some favourite toys and games, a bucket and spade for the beach and Edward, the teddy that Joe always took to bed with him.

Put a ring round the correct answer.

✶ Joe's teddy was called   **Edmund.**

Edward.

Edwina.

Edith.

✶ The story is set in

the spring.   **the summer.**   **the autumn.**   **the winter.**

© Andrew Brodie Publications ✓ www.acblack.com

| YEAR 2 | UNIT 2 | Sheet B | Name _____ | Joe and his Grandad |

Joe and his Grandad - Part 2

It was a wonderful week for Joe. On Sunday Grandad took Joe to the beach for a picnic. They paddled in the water, dug holes in the sand and made a magnificent sandcastle. The castle had four towers, a moat round the edge and was decorated with shells. Joe and Grandad finished the day with large creamy ice-creams, which they ate on the way home.

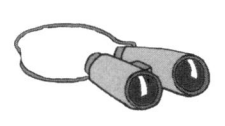

The next day they went for a walk in the countryside, and Grandad let Joe use his binoculars to look at birds and butterflies.

On Tuesday morning Grandad played cricket in the garden with Joe. In the afternoon they went to the shops as Grandad needed to do some food shopping.

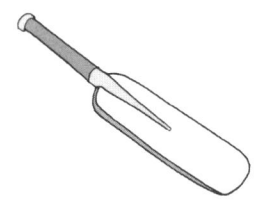

★ What did Joe use to look at birds?

binoculars   **glasses**   **telescope**

★ What was used to decorate the sandcastle?

stones   **shells**   **flags**   **moat**

★ What did Joe and Grandad do on Monday?

_____

_____

★ Which word in the text describes the sandcastle?

_____

© Andrew Brodie Publications ✓ www.acblack.com

Joe and his Grandad - Part 3

Wednesday and Thursday were both rather cool rainy days, so Joe and Grandad played with some of Joe's favourite games. As a special treat, Grandad took Joe to the cinema on Thursday after tea.

On Friday the sun was shining and the weather was warm. Joe and Grandad visited a small wildlife park that day. They saw monkeys (Grandad said they looked just like a little boy he knew), tigers, snakes, crocodiles and many other creatures.

✱ Which days were cool and rainy?

- [ ] **Saturday and Sunday**
- [ ] **Tuesday and Wednesday**
- [ ] **Monday and Tuesday**
- [ ] **Wednesday and Thursday**

✱ On which day did Joe and Grandad visit the Wildlife Park?

- [ ] **Tuesday** - [ ] **Sunday** - [ ] **Monday** - [ ] **Friday**

✱ Who do you think Grandad meant when he said the monkeys reminded him of a little boy he knew?

_____

_____

| YEAR 2 | UNIT 3 | Sheet B | Name _____ Joe and his Grandad

Joe and his Grandad - Part 4

Saturday was Joe's last full day at Grandad's house, and Joe was allowed to choose what he would like to do. He thought carefully, and decided that he wanted to go to the beach again, so off they went.

Mum and Dad came to collect Joe on Sunday. He was sad to leave Grandad's house, but pleased to see his parents again. Joe slept soundly on the journey home. He had enjoyed a busy week at Grandad's house, and was hoping he would be able to go there again the next summer.

∗ Did Mum and Dad stay at Grandad's too? _____

∗ What was Joe's favourite activity when he went to stay with Grandad?

_____

_____

∗ How do you know that?

_____

_____

On the back of the sheet draw or write about something you would like to do during the next school holiday.

© Andrew Brodie Publications ✓ www.acblack.com

This unit addresses the Literacy Strategy:
Term 1, 2, 3 objective 1: to reinforce and apply their word-level skills through shared and guided reading.
Term 1, 2, 3 objective 2: to use phonological, contextual, grammatical and graphic knowledge to work out, predict, and check the meanings of unfamiliar words and to make sense of what they read.
You may also find it helpful when covering :
Term 1 objective 4: to understand time and sequential relationships in stories, i.e. what happened when.

YEAR 2 | UNIT 4 | Sheet A

Name _____ Abbie's Parcel

Abbie's Parcel

This story is written in 4 parts but they are printed in the wrong order. Read each part and put them in the correct order.

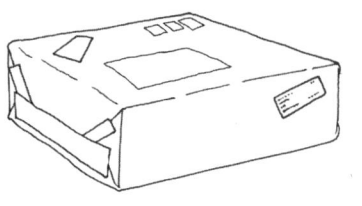

Part 1	Now she was feeling better. She pulled back the curtains and saw the lovely day for herself. She trotted downstairs to see who had sent her a parcel.
Part 2	Abbie lay in bed with the sun peeping through the curtains. The birds were singing as if they were telling her what a lovely day it was. Abbie hated getting up. "Get up Abbie," called Mum.
Part 3	It was from London. She had entered a colouring competition weeks ago and she had won! The prize was a camera with 2 films. It was certainly worth getting up today.
Part 4	Abbie put one foot out of bed and then the other. She walked slowly to the bathroom, to wash her face and then back to her bedroom to put on her clothes. "Abbie, there's a parcel for you. Hurry up," said Mum.

Write the correct order of the parts here.

Beginning of story			End of story

© Andrew Brodie Publications ✓ www.acblack.com

YEAR	UNIT	Sheet
2	4	B

Name   Abbie's Parcel

Here is a copy of the story in the correct sequence.

Abbie lay in bed with the sun peeping through the curtains. The birds were singing as if they were telling her what a lovely day it was. Abbie hated getting up.

"Get up Abbie," called Mum.

Abbie put one foot out of bed and then the other. She walked slowly to the bathroom, to wash her face and then back to her bedroom to put on her clothes.

"Abbie, there's a parcel for you. Hurry up," said Mum.

Now she was feeling better. She pulled back the curtains and saw the lovely day for herself. She trotted downstairs to see who had sent her a parcel.

It was from London. She had entered a colouring competition weeks ago and she had won! The prize was a camera with 2 films. It was certainly worth getting up today.

1. At the start of the story Abbie was

   ☐ in the bathroom.   ☐ in the kitchen.

   ☐ in her bedroom.   ☐ in the garden.

2. What did Abbie feel about getting up?

   ☐ She liked it.   ☐ She hated it.

3. What made Abbie feel better?

   _____

   _____

4. What was in her parcel?

   _____

   _____

© Andrew Brodie Publications ✓ www.acblack.com

This unit addresses the Literacy Strategy:
Term 1, 2, 3 objective   1: to reinforce and apply their word-level skills through shared and guided reading.
Term 1, 2, 3 objective   2: to use phonological, contextual, grammatical and graphic knowledge to work out, predict, and check the meanings of unfamiliar words and to make sense of what they read.
You may also find it helpful when covering :
Term 1 objective 4:   to understand time and sequential relationships in stories, i.e. what happened when.

| YEAR 2 | UNIT 5 | Sheet A |

Name   Using the Computer

Using the Computer

Amil was the last person to go on the computer yesterday. He played a spelling game on it.

Before Amil it was Kate, who did some adding questions. She was on the computer for most of the afternoon.

Sam was on it before Kate. He used the mouse to draw a picture. It had lots of colours.

Yesterday morning, Jasdeep started the day at the computer. She drew a picture of a cat.

After Jasdeep, Tom used the computer. He wrote a sentence.

The last person to use the computer yesterday morning was Sara. She played a spelling game.

© Andrew Brodie Publications ✓ www.acblack.com

YEAR	UNIT	Sheet
2	5	B

Name _____ Using the Computer

☐ Who was the very **first** person to use the computer yesterday? ☐

☐ Who was the **second** person? ☐

☐ Who was the **third**? ☐

☐ Who was the **fourth**? ☐

☐ Who was the **fifth**? ☐

☐ Who was the last person to use the computer yesterday? ☐

☐ Who played a spelling game?

☐ _____ and _____

☐ Who drew pictures?

☐ _____ and _____

Write sentences to answer these questions.

☐ What did Tom do?

_____

_____

☐ What did Kate do?

_____

_____

© Andrew Brodie Publications ✓ www.acblack.com

This unit addresses the Literacy Strategy:
Term 1, 2, 3 objective   1: to reinforce and apply their word-level skills through shared and guided reading.
Term 1, 2, 3 objective   2: to use phonological, contextual, grammatical and graphic knowledge to work out, predict, and check the meanings of unfamiliar words and to make sense of what they read.
You may also find it helpful when covering :
Term 1 objective   4: to understand time and sequential relationships in stories, i.e what happened when.
Term 1 objective   5: to identify and discuss reasons for events in stories, linked to plot.

YEAR 2 UNIT 6 Sheet A   Name   Kim's Holiday Journey

Kim's Holiday Journey

Kim sat on the train looking out of the window.

Mum was cross and Dad was cross because the train was late.

The train arrived at the station. Mum cheered up and Dad cheered up.

They got off the train and went out of the station.

They found a taxi and went to their caravan.

"On holiday at last," said Kim.

© Andrew Brodie Publications ✓ www.acblack.com

Year	Unit	Sheet
2	6	B

Name _____   Kim's Holiday Journey

Find the answers to the questions.

Put a tick by the right answer.

1. Kim was travelling on a

   ...plane. ☐   ...boat. ☐

   ...bike. ☐   ...train. ☐

2. Why were Mum and Dad cross?

   Mum and Dad were cross because   **...Kim was naughty.** ☐

   ...the train was late. ☐

   ...the train arrived. ☐

3. Where were Mum, Dad and Kim going?

   Mum, Dad and Kim were going   **... on holiday.** ☐

   ... home. ☐

   ...to an airport. ☐

4. They were going to stay

   ...at a hotel. ☐

   ... with friends. ☐

   ... in a caravan. ☐

© Andrew Brodie Publications   ✓   www.acblack.com

This unit addresses the Literacy Strategy:
Term 1, 2, 3 objective   1: to reinforce and apply their word-level skills through shared and guided reading.
Term 1, 2, 3 objective   2: to use phonological, contextual, grammatical and graphic knowledge to work out, predict, and check the meanings of unfamiliar words and to make sense of what they read.
You may also find it helpful when covering :
Term 1 objective   5: to identify and discuss reasons for events in stories, linked to plot.
Term 2 objective   4: to predict story endings/incidents, e.g. from unfinished extracts, while reading with the teacher.

YEAR 2 | UNIT 7 | Sheet A

Name

Sally and the Robin (Part 1)

Sally and the Robin (Part 1)

Sally was watching a robin in the garden. It was hopping about on the grass, looking for worms. Then it flew into the cherry tree, which was covered in pink spring blossom.

Sally often stood watching the robin from her bedroom window.

The bird flew down onto the flower bed. Sally was about to turn away when she saw a cat creeping slowly, silently towards the robin. There seemed to be no sound at all and Sally knew that the cat was about to pounce.

What was robin looking for?

☐ **Sally**   ☐ **worms**   ☐ **a cherry**   ☐ **a cat**

How do you think Sally knew that the cat was going to pounce?

_____

_____

What do you think Sally did next?

_____

_____

What would you do if you were Sally?

_____

_____

© Andrew Brodie Publications ✓ www.acblack.com

| YEAR 2 | UNIT 7 | Sheet B | Name

Sally and the Robin (Part 2)

Sally and the Robin (Part 2)

"Go away!" shouted Sally, opening her window, "Shoo!" The robin flew to the safety of the tree. The cat looked crossly at Sally and sat down.

Sally searched around her bedroom. In a box under her bed she found a ball that she hadn't played with for a long time and an old skipping rope.

She went out into the garden and could see the cat looking into the cherry tree to find the robin. Sally thought that if she played with the cat he wouldn't try to catch the robin.

She ran around the garden, pulling the rope behind her, with the cat chasing the end as if it was a mouse. After that Sally rolled the ball for the cat to run after.

At last, the cat curled up in the sun to go to sleep.

"The robin is safe for now," thought Sally.

Who moved when Sally shouted?   ☐ the cat   ☐ the robin

Why did Sally find an old rope and a ball?

☐ to play with on her own   ☐ for the cat to play with

Why did Sally play with the cat?

_____

_____

© Andrew Brodie Publications ✓ www.acblack.com

This unit addresses the Literacy Strategy:
Term 1, 2, 3 objective 1: to reinforce and apply their word-level skills through shared and guided reading.
Term 1, 2, 3 objective 2: to use phonological, contextual, grammatical and graphic knowledge to work out, predict, and check the meanings of unfamiliar words and to make sense of what they read.
You may also find it helpful when covering :
Term 1 objective 5: to identify and discuss reasons for events in stories, linked to plot.
Term 1 objective 7: to learn, reread and recite favourite poems, taking account of punctuation; to comment on aspects such as word combinations, sound patterns (such as rhymes, rhythms, alliterative patterns) and forms of presentation.

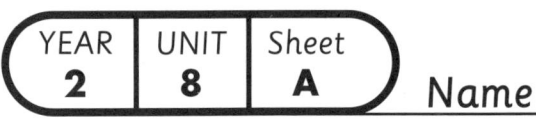

YEAR 2 | UNIT 8 | Sheet A

Name

Tom and Tim's Mishap

Tom and Tim's Mishap

Tom and Tim went to the hall.

Tom and Tim threw a ball.

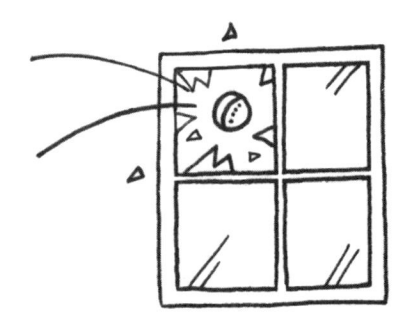

Tom and Tim broke some glass.

Tom and Tim went back to class.

Tom and Tim have been bad.

Tom and Tim are very sad.

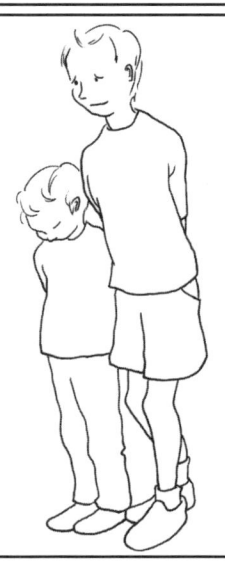

© Andrew Brodie Publications ✓ www.acblack.com

| YEAR 2 | UNIT 8 | Sheet B | Name _____ | Tom and Tim's Mishap |

Answer the questions.

Use the words from the word bank.

WORD BANK
ball   window
Tom   teacher
sad   Tim

1. What were the names of the boys?

   [_____] and [_____]

2. What did the boys throw? [_____]

3. What did they break? [_____]

4. Who do you think was cross with the boys? [_____]

5. How did the boys feel? [_____]

What do you think happened next?

_____
_____
_____
_____
_____

This unit addresses the Literacy Strategy:
Term 1, 2, 3 objective   1: to reinforce and apply their word-level skills through shared and guided reading.
Term 1, 2, 3 objective   2: to use phonological, contextual, grammatical and graphic knowledge to work out, predict, and check the meanings of unfamiliar words and to make sense of what they read.
You may also find it helpful when covering:
Term 2 objective 14: to note key structural features, e.g. clear statement of purpose at start, sequential steps set out in a list, direct language.
Term 3 objective 13: to understand the distinction between fact and fiction; to use terms 'fact', 'fiction' and 'non-fiction' appropriately.

YEAR 2 | UNIT 9 | Sheet A   Name   Department Stores

Department Stores

Most towns have at least one department store. This is a shop that sells a wide variety of goods with an area, or department, for each type of thing for sale.

A typical department store might sell clothes, books, toys, furniture, towels, bed linen, kitchen equipment, stationery, gifts and many other things too. Many large department stores are on several floors, with stairs, lifts or escalators to help customers to go from one floor to the next.

On each floor there is usually a 'store guide' to help customers to find the department they are looking for. Read the store guide at the bottom on this page to help you to answer some of the questions on the next one.

Basement	Travel Goods / Sports Wear
Ground Floor	Gifts / Kitchenware / Home Furnishings
First Floor	Bed Linen / Towels / Curtains / Clothing
Second Floor	Toys / Books / Restaurant / Toilet

© Andrew Brodie Publications ✓ www.acblack.com

| YEAR 2 | UNIT 9 | Sheet B | Name _____ | Department Stores |

Answer the questions carefully.

You may need a dictionary.

Tick the correct answers.

Is a 'department store' another name for a bookshop?
☐ Yes   ☐ No

Would you expect to find a department store in a very small village?
☐ Yes   ☐ No

Which of the following words mean a moving staircase?
☐ lift   ☐ escalator   ☐ elevator

Which word in the text means the same as shop?
☐ typical   ☐ store   ☐ goods   ☐ department

In which department would you find paper and envelopes?
☐ toy   ☐ bed linen   ☐ furniture   ☐ stationery

Is the text fiction or non-fiction?
☐ fiction   ☐ non-fiction

Now look at the store guide to write the answer to the next four questions.

On which floor would you find the toy department? _____

Where would you go to buy a suitcase? _____

On which floor could you buy some lunch? _____

Name two of the departments on the ground floor.

_____   _____

© Andrew Brodie Publications ✓ www.acblack.com

This unit addresses the Literacy Strategy:
Term 1, 2, 3 objective   1: to reinforce and apply their word-level skills through shared and guided reading.
Term 1, 2, 3 objective   2: to use phonological, contextual, grammatical and graphic knowledge to work out, predict, and check the meanings of unfamiliar words and to make sense of what they read.
You may also find it helpful when covering :
Term 1 objective 13: to read simple written instructions in the classroom, simple recipes, plans, instructions for constructing something.

YEAR 2 | UNIT 10 | Sheet A

Name _____   Making a Tepee

Making a Model Tepee From Card

Native American Indians lived in tents called tepees. They were made from animal skins and were decorated with paintings of the things they saw around them.

Follow these instructions to make a model tepee from the template.

1. Decorate the tepee using crayons or felt tips before you cut it out.

2. Cut around the edge of the thick black lines. (Don't cut off the tab - it is important.)

3. Fold along the dotted lines. _ _ _ _

4. Put glue along the tab and stick it under the other long straight edge to make a tent shape.

5. You can put your tepee with your classmates' tepees to make an Indian village.

You could find out more about Native American Indians in the library or by looking on the computer.

© Andrew Brodie Publications ✓ www.acblack.com

| YEAR 2 | UNIT 10 | Sheet B | Name | Making a Tepee |

A model tepee to make.

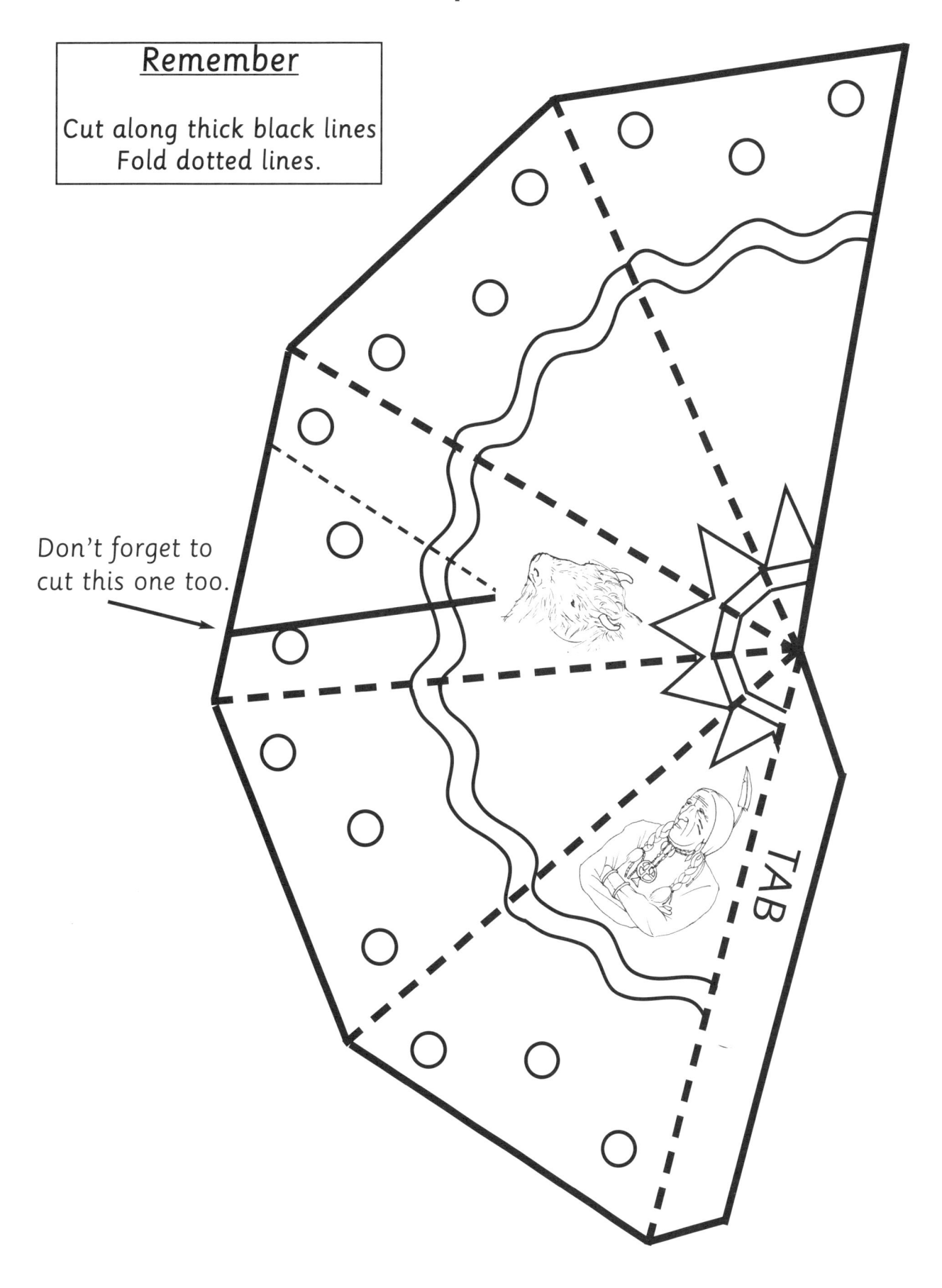

Note: Photocopy on to thin card.

Remember

Cut along thick black lines
Fold dotted lines.

Don't forget to cut this one too.

TAB

© Andrew Brodie Publications ✓ www.acblack.com

This unit addresses the Literacy Strategy:
Term 1, 2, 3 objective 1: to reinforce and apply their word-level skills through shared and guided reading.
Term 1, 2, 3 objective 2: to use phonological, contextual, grammatical and graphic knowledge to work out, predict, and check the meanings of unfamiliar words and to make sense of what they read.
You may also find it helpful when covering :
Term 1 objective 14: to note key structural features, e.g. clear statement of purpose at start, sequential steps set out in a list, direct language.

| YEAR 2 | UNIT 11 | Sheet A |

Name   Crossing the Road Safely

Crossing the Road Safely

Follow these five steps to cross the road safely.

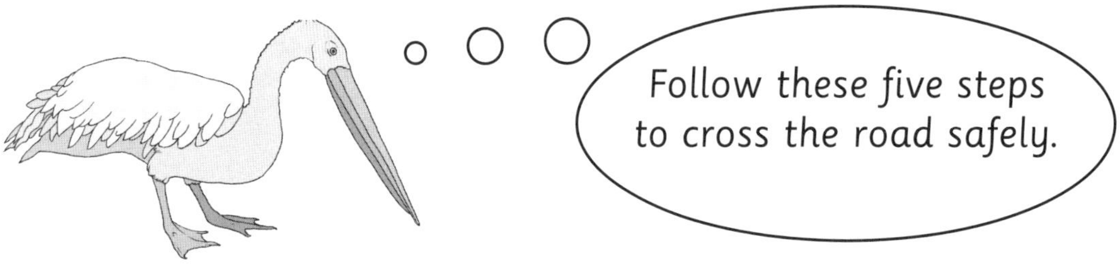

1. **Find a safe place to cross the road.**
   Never cross near parked cars, near the brow of a hill or near a bend in the road.
   Use a proper crossing place if there is one.
   Zebra crossings and pelican crossings are the safest places.

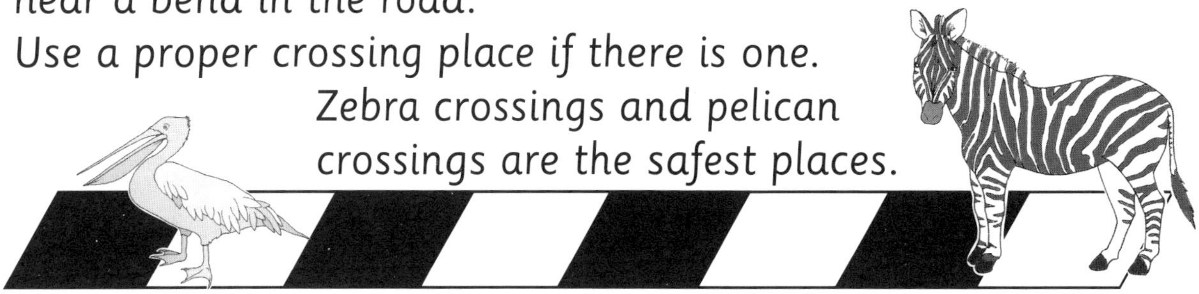

2. **Stand near the kerb.**
   Be close enough to see along the road, but do not stand on the very edge as it could be dangerous.

3. **Look both ways and listen.**
   Listening is very important. Sometimes you can hear traffic before you can see it.

4. **Wait until the road is clear.**
   Let all traffic go past.
   Wait until you cannot see or hear any traffic.

5. **Walk across the road.**
   Always walk straight to the other side.
   Keep looking and listening as you walk.
   Never run across the road.

© Andrew Brodie Publications ✓ www.acblack.com

YEAR	UNIT	Sheet
2	11	B

Name _____ Crossing the Road Safely

Do you cross the road safely?

I always use the pelican crossing.

Tick the correct answers.

🚗 Where should you cross the road?

☐ on the side of a hill ☐ near a bend
☐ behind a parked car ☐ in a safe place

🚗 Instruction number four tells you to

☐ skip across the road. ☐ wait until the road is clear.
☐ stand near the kerb. ☐ walk across the road.

🚗 Where should you stand when waiting to cross the road?

☐ in the gutter ☐ on the kerb
☐ near the kerb ☐ in the road

Write the correct answer to these questions.

🚗 Why should you listen for traffic as well as look?

_____

_____

🚗 Why do the instructions have numbers?

_____

_____

_____

🚗 Name two safe places to cross the road.

_____

_____

Design a bold colourful poster to show people how to cross the road safely.

© Andrew Brodie Publications ✓ www.acblack.com

This unit addresses the Literacy Strategy:
Term 1, 2, 3 objective   1: to reinforce and apply their word-level skills through shared and guided reading.
Term 1, 2, 3 objective   2: to use phonological, contextual, grammatical and graphic knowledge to work out, predict, and check the meanings of unfamiliar words and to make sense of what they read.
You may also find it helpful when covering :
Term 1 objective 4:   to understand time and sequential relationships in stories, i.e. what happened when.
Term 2 objective 4:   to predict story endings/incidents, e.g. from unfinished extracts, while reading with the teacher.

YEAR 2 | UNIT 12 | Sheet A   Name   Jamie's Puppy

Jamie's Puppy

When Jamie woke up that morning he was very excited. It was his birthday. He was seven years old and was hoping that today he might be getting the pet he had always wanted - a puppy. Not a pretend cuddle puppy like the one he took to bed with him each night, but a real live puppy to look after and love.

Jamie rushed downstairs where a small pile of presents and cards were waiting. Firstly he opened a shirt from grandma and grandad, next a computer game from Aunty Sue, after that an art set from Uncle Bill and lastly some money from his cousin Josh.

He was delighted with his gifts, but where, oh where, could a dog be?

"Oh by the way Jamie, there is another small present in the kitchen," smiled Mum.

Jamie ran through to the kitchen and there, curled up in a small basket in the corner, was a soft, furry, brown puppy, sound asleep.

"Wow!" said Jamie, going towards the peaceful animal.

"Wait," whispered mum, "let him sleep. He is sure to wake up soon, and while you are waiting you can begin to read this book on how to look after him. It's very important to look after a pet properly to keep him happy, healthy and well behaved."

© Andrew Brodie Publications ✓ www.acblack.com

| YEAR 2 | UNIT 12 | Sheet B | Name | Jamie's Puppy |

Use the story of Jamie's Puppy to help you answer the questions. Ring the correct answer.

What did Jamie take to bed with him at night?

    a book   **a drink**   **a teddy**   **a toy dog**

Who bought Jamie a computer game?

    Grandma   **Aunty Sue**   **Josh**   **Uncle Bill**

Where did Jamie find the puppy?

    bathroom   **kitchen**   **porch**   **bedroom**

Write the answer to these questions.

How did Jamie feel when he woke up on his seventh birthday?

_____

_____

Which word in the story tells us how Jamie went down the stairs? [ ]

What did Mum want Jamie to do while he was waiting for the puppy to wake up?

_____

_____

Why did she want him to do this?

_____

_____

What do you think Jamie did when the puppy woke up?

_____

_____

© Andrew Brodie Publications ✓ www.acblack.com

This unit addresses the Literacy Strategy:
Term 1, 2, 3 objective   1: to reinforce and apply their word-level skills through shared and guided reading.
Term 1, 2, 3 objective   2: to use phonological, contextual, grammatical and graphic knowledge to work out, predict, and check the meanings of unfamiliar words and to make sense of what they read.
You may also find it helpful when covering :
Term 1 objective 4:   to understand time and sequential relationships in stories, i.e. what happened when.
Term 2 objective 4:   to predict story endings/incidents, e.g. from unfinished extracts, while reading with the teacher.

YEAR 2 | UNIT 13 | Sheet A   Name _____   Young Frog (Part 1)

Young Frog (Part 1)

Young Frog was excited. All his legs had grown and he was ready to leap out of the pond for the very first time. He crawled slowly out of the water onto a large lily leaf. Then, before he had time to think, he leapt....up, up, up and over the edge of the pond onto the grass. For the first time in his life he was on dry land!

Young Frog leapt again and again, all around the edge of the pond. Then he stopped to look at two tall sticks. At the top of the sticks was a feathery body...and at the top of the feathery body was a long feathery neck...and at the top of the feathery neck was a feathery head with two beady eyes and a long, sharp beak.

"Hello, Young Frog," said Tall Heron. "You look very tasty!"

Young Frog did not stop to say "hello". He turned around and leapt back into the pond. He hid under a lily leaf for a moment but slowly crawled on top of it, ready to leap out again.

© Andrew Brodie Publications ✓ www.acblack.com

YEAR	UNIT	Sheet
2	13	B

Name   Young Frog (Part 1)

Young Frog (Part 1)

1. Young Frog was excited because
   ☐ he met a heron.   ☐ he jumped into the pond.
   ☐ he liked lilies.   ☐ he could leap out of the pond.

2. What did Young Frog climb onto first?
   _____
   _____

3. What do you think Tall Heron was going to do to Young Frog?
   _____
   _____

4. Why did Young Frog leap back into the pond?
   ☐ To hide from heron.   ☐ It was wet.
   ☐ His friends were there.   ☐ He could say "hello".

What do you think happened next in the story? Who did Young Frog see this time? Write the second part of the story yourself and then read Young Frog (Part 2) to find another ending.

© Andrew Brodie Publications ✓ www.acblack.com

This unit addresses the Literacy Strategy:
Term 1, 2, 3 objective 1: to reinforce and apply their word-level skills through shared and guided reading.
Term 1, 2, 3 objective 2: to use phonological, contextual, grammatical and graphic knowledge to work out, predict, and check the meanings of unfamiliar words and to make sense of what they read.
You may also find it helpful when covering :
Term 1 objective 4:   to understand time and sequential relationships in stories, i.e. what happened when.
Term 2 objective 4:   to predict story endings/incidents, e.g. from unfinished extracts, while reading with the teacher.

YEAR 2 | UNIT 14 | Sheet A   Name   Young Frog (Part 2)

Young Frog (Part 2)

Young Frog sat on the lily pad and had a good look around. There was no sign of Tall Heron and everything was quiet. Two people were fishing at the far end of the pond, so he wouldn't go that way.

Just then a young rabbit's ears appeared in the grass.

"He looks friendly," thought Young Frog. So he took a huge leap in the direction of the rabbit.

"Hello," said Young Frog. "This is only the second time I have been out of the pond."

"Hello," said Rabbit. "Do you live in the pond? You must get very wet!"

"Yes," replied Young Frog. "When I was a tadpole I stayed in there all the time but now I'm a frog I can come on land too."

"Do you want to see where I live? It's just over there," said Rabbit, pointing with his nose.

"Yes please," said Young Frog.

Rabbit took him to a smooth hole in the bank. Young Frog thought it looked a very strange dark place to live but he was too polite to say so.

"That's nice," he said instead.

Frog thought he would much rather live in his pond with all his brothers and sisters and play on the lily pads.

Young Frog said good-bye to Rabbit and jumped back to the pond. He felt he had had an adventure but it was good to be home.

| YEAR 2 | UNIT 14 | Sheet B |

Name   Young Frog (Part 2)

Young Frog (Part 2)

1. Why do you think Young Frog had a good look around when he was on the lily pad ready to leap out of the pond?

    ☐ because he was nosy

    ☐ to sit in the sun

    ☐ to make sure it was safe

2. Another name for lily pad is:

    ☐ lily stem   ☐ lily flower

    ☐ lily leaf   ☐ lily root

3. Put these events in the order that they happened in the story. Number them from 1 to 5.

    ☐ He said "Hello" to Rabbit.

    ☐ Young Frog went back to his pond.

    ☐ Young Frog jumped out of the pond.

    ☐ Rabbit took Young Frog to his hole.

    ☐ Young Frog sat on a lily pad and looked around.

Write a new adventure for Young Frog. Who could he meet next?

This unit addresses the Literacy Strategy:
Term 1, 2, 3 objective   1: to reinforce and apply their word-level skills through shared and guided reading.
Term 1, 2, 3 objective   2: to use phonological, contextual, grammatical and graphic knowledge to work out, predict, and check the meanings of unfamiliar words and to make sense of what they read.
You may also find it helpful when covering:
Term 2 objective   5: to discuss story settings: to compare differences; to locate key words and phrases in text; to consider how different settings influence events and behaviour.
Term 2 objective   6: to identify and describe characters, expressing own views and using words and phrases from texts.

YEAR 2 | UNIT 15 | Sheet A   Name   The Two Jays

The Two Jays

The playground was a large bustling place, full of children laughing and playing. They all seemed very happy to be there, knowing each other and greeting their friends. All that is, except Jay.

Jay had just arrived at the school and was feeling very lonely, frightened and very very new. He had a new school uniform, a new school bag, a new PE kit and a new lunch box.

A whistle blew and all the children became quiet and formed neat lines. Jay was feeling empty and alone; he didn't know where to go. He could feel tears forming in his eyes. He tried to blink them away and then wiped his face with his sleeve, his very new sleeve.

"Hi," a voice said cheerfully. It was another boy about his own age. "You must be Jay."

"Yes," replied Jay, surprised that someone seemed to know him.

"Our teacher told us you were starting today," said the other boy, "and it's my job to make sure you have a friend for the day. By the way, my name's Jay."

"So is mine," said Jay and they both laughed.

By the end of the day they were best of friends and soon became known as "The Two Jays". Jay knew then that he was going to be very happy at his new school.

© Andrew Brodie Publications ✓ www.acblack.com

| YEAR 2 | UNIT 15 | Sheet B |

Name   The Two Jays

> Use 'The Two Jays' to help you to answer the questions.

Tick the correct answer.

1. Who was feeling lonely?

    the teacher   **Joy**   **Jay**   **Jim**

2. Which word in the text means the same as **bustling**?

    lonely   **busy**   **laughing**   **playground**

Write the answer to these questions.

3. What is the title of the story?
   _____

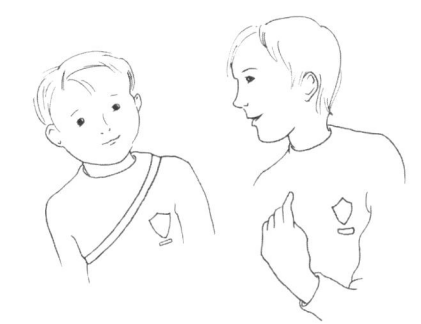

4. Why do you think the author chose that title?
   _____
   _____

5. Write another good title for the story.
   _____

6. How do you think Jay felt at the beginning of the story?
   _____
   _____

7. How do you think he felt at the end of the story?
   _____
   _____

8. Why did his feelings change?
   _____
   _____

© Andrew Brodie Publications ✓ www.acblack.com

This unit addresses the Literacy Strategy:
Term 1, 2, 3 objective   1: to reinforce and apply their word-level skills through shared and guided reading.
Term 1, 2, 3 objective   2: to use phonological, contextual, grammatical and graphic knowledge to work out, predict, and check the meanings of unfamiliar words and to make sense of what they read.
You may also find it helpful when covering :
Term 2 objective 8:   to read own poems aloud.
Term 2 objective 9:   to identify and discuss patterns of rhythm, rhyme and other features of sound in different poems.

YEAR 2 | UNIT 16 | Sheet A

Name   Toad Poem

Toad Poem

1. On the next page is a poem about a toad. Some of the rhyming words are missing from the end of each line. Try to find a rhyming word to fit in each space.

2. Some of the lines have speech marks around them. Who is speaking these lines? Tick the correct answer.

   ☐ **the person walking down the road**

   ☐ **the toad**

3. What magic do you think the toad could do?

   _____

   _____

4. Write one more pair of rhyming lines to finish the poem in the space provided.

5. Give the poem a title.

6. Practise reading your finished poem, either by yourself or with a partner.

© Andrew Brodie Publications ✓ www.acblack.com

| Year 2 | Unit 16 | Sheet B |

Name   Toad Poem

Name _____ Date _____

Title _____

As I was walking down the [   ]
I stepped beside a great big toad!

He looked at me and shook his fist,
"You are very lucky that you [   ]."

"If you had trodden on my [   ]
What would have happened no-one knows."

"I wave this wand to make some [   ]
The consequence can be most tragic."

_____

_____

© Andrew Brodie Publications ✓ www.acblack.com

This unit addresses the Literacy Strategy:
Term 1, 2, 3 objective 1: to reinforce and apply their word-level skills through shared and guided reading.
Term 1, 2, 3 objective 2: to use phonological, contextual, grammatical and graphic knowledge to work out, predict, and check the meanings of unfamiliar words and to make sense of what they read.
Term 2 objective 9: to identify and discuss patterns of rhythm, rhyme and other features of sound in different poems.
Term 2 objective 10: to comment on and recognise when the reading aloud of a poem makes sense and is effective.

YEAR 2 | UNIT 17 | Sheet A | Name | What David Saw

What David Saw

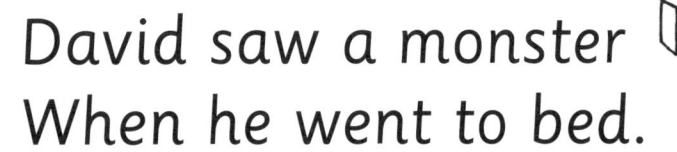

David saw a monster
When he went to bed.
"There's not one in the wardrobe,"
His angel mummy said.

"There's not one in the bathroom,
There's not one in the loo.
There's not one in the house at all
To frighten me and you."

David saw an angel
When he went to bed.
"Monsters are just creatures
That live inside your head."

© Andrew Brodie Publications ✓ www.acblack.com

YEAR	UNIT	Sheet
2	17	B

Name _____   What David Saw

Read the poem out loud.

1. Which two words rhyme in the first verse?

   ☐   ☐

2. Which two words rhyme in the second verse?

   ☐   ☐

3. Which two words rhyme in the third verse?

   ☐   ☐

4. Who made David feel better?

   ☐

5. Where did Mummy look for monsters?

   Mummy looked for monsters _____
   _____
   _____

6. Were the monsters real?   ☐

7. Where did Mummy say the monsters were?

   Mummy said the monsters were _____
   _____
   _____

© Andrew Brodie Publications ✓ www.acblack.com

Dressing Up

I dream of fine clothing to dress in each day.
I love to dress up and pretend when I play.
I could wear a sari, so pink and so bright,
Edged with deep blue, like the clear sky at night.

Perhaps sparkling jewels would make me look fine.
A necklace of rubies and pearls could be mine.
Maybe the head-wear, of bride or of groom,
Or a helmet to take a spaceman to the moon.

I could dress as a butcher or baker maybe,
Or a chef cooking chips and some cake for my tea.
The clothes of a rider, straight backed on a horse,
Jumping the fences around the racecourse.

Wellies on feet, or slides in my hair,
Shoes made for dancing, and ice skates, a pair.
But I can't wear these yet, because now instead
I must put on pyjamas and get into bed!

| YEAR 2 | UNIT 18 | Sheet B |

Name   Dressing Up

Ring the correct answer to these questions.

✻ What is the title of the poem?

   I Dream   **Dressing Up**   **Fine Clothing**

✻ In the poem, what is made of rubies and pearls?

   necklace   **bracelet**   **ring**   **crown**

✻ Which word in verse three, rhymes with horse?

   house   **tea**   **racecourse**   **force**

✻ Who in verse two wears a helmet?

   fireman   **policeman**   **spaceman**

Write the correct answer to these questions.

✻ What might the chef be cooking?

_____

_____

✻ What word describes the jewels in verse two? _____

✻ What time of day do you think it is in the poem?

_____

✻ Why do you think this? _____

_____

On the back of the sheet draw and colour a picture of you in some clothes you would like to dress up in.

© Andrew Brodie Publications ✓ www.acblack.com

This unit addresses the Literacy Strategy:
Term 1, 2, 3 objective   1: to reinforce and apply their word-level skills through shared and guided reading.
Term 1, 2, 3 objective   2: to use phonological, contextual, grammatical and graphic knowledge to work out, predict, and check the meanings of unfamiliar words and to make sense of what they read.
You may also find it helpful when covering :
Term 2 objective 16: to use dictionaries and glossaries to locate words by using initial letter.
Term 2 objective 17: that dictionaries and glossaries give definitions and explanations; discuss what definitions are, explore some simple definitions in dictionaries.

YEAR 2 | UNIT 19 | Sheet A   Name   The Glossary

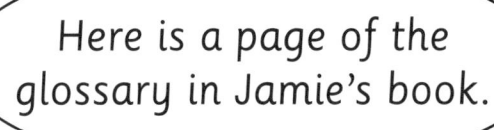

Here is a page of the glossary in Jamie's book.

A glossary is a list of words and their meanings. It helps the reader to understand the book.

Kennel	A strong outdoor home suitable for a dog to sleep in.
Mongrel	A dog that cannot be identified as any named breed. These dogs often make extremely good pets.
Pedigree	A particular breed of dog that comes from a family of that breed.
Puppy	A young dog is known as a puppy until it is a fully grown adult.
Terrier	Terriers are breeds of dog that are good at digging. These include West Highland Terriers, Scottish Terriers and Yorkshire Terriers.
Toy Dogs	These are very small breeds of dog. They will grow to about 30 centimetres high when fully grown, and can be even smaller than this.
Wolf	All modern dogs that we have as pets are descendants of the wolf.

© Andrew Brodie Publications ✓ www.acblack.com

YEAR	UNIT	Sheet
2	19	B

Name

The Glossary

Answer these questions carefully.

Some only need a word, and others need a whole sentence.

Questions about the Glossary in Jamie's Book.

Name one example of a terrier.

In what special order are the words in the glossary set out?

_____

_____

What is a young dog called?

What outdoor building might a dog sleep in?

What is a very small breed of dog known as?

What are all terriers very good at doing?

All our modern pet dogs are descendants of which wild animal?

In your own words write a sentence to explain what a mongrel is.

_____

_____

On the back of the sheet draw or write a list of all the things you think you would need to care for a dog properly. Here are two things to start you off.

Identity tag

Collar

© Andrew Brodie Publications ✓ www.acblack.com

This unit addresses the Literacy Strategy:
Term 1, 2, 3 objective 1: to reinforce and apply their word-level skills through shared and guided reading.
Term 1, 2, 3 objective 2: to use phonological, contextual, grammatical and graphic knowledge to work out, predict, and check the meanings of unfamiliar words and to make sense of what they read.
You may also find it helpful when covering :
Term 1 objective 7: to learn, reread and recite favourite poems, taking account of punctuation; to comment on aspects such as word combinations, sound patterns (such as rhymes, rhythms, alliterative patterns) and forms of presentation.
Term 1 objective 8: to collect and categorise poems to build class anthologies.
Term 2 objective 11: to identify and discuss favourite poems, using appropriate terms (poet, poem, verse, rhyme, etc) and referring to the language of the poems.
Term 3 objective 6: to read, respond imaginatively, recommend and collect examples of humourous stories, extracts, poems.
Term 3 objective 8: to discuss meanings of words and phrases that create humour, and sound effects in poetry, e.g. nonsense poems, tongue-twisters, riddles, and to classify poems into simple types; to make class anthologies.

YEAR 2 | UNIT 20 | Sheet A

Name _____ The Owl and the Pussy-cat

The Owl and the Pussy-cat

This is a nonsense poem.

It couldn't really have happened, but it's fun to read.

The Owl and the Pussy-cat went to sea
In a beautiful pea-green boat,
They took some honey, and plenty of money,
Wrapped up in a five-pound note.
The Owl looked up to the stars above,
And sang to a small guitar,
'O lovely Pussy! O Pussy my love,
What a beautiful Pussy you are,
    You are,
    You are!
What a beautiful Pussy you are!'

by Edward Lear

Which word in this verse rhymes with note?

☐ above   ☐ boat   ☐ love   ☐ money

© Andrew Brodie Publications ✓ www.acblack.com

| YEAR 2 | UNIT 20 | Sheet B | Name _____ | The Owl and the Pussy-cat |

What instrument did Owl play?

☐ **banjo**   ☐ **drum**   ☐ **triangle**   ☐ **guitar**

Write a sentence to answer each of these questions.

Who wrote 'The Owl and the Pussy-cat' poem?
_____
_____
_____

What word does Owl use in verse one to describe Pussy?
_____
_____
_____

Now read the second verse.

Pussy said to the Owl, 'You elegant fowl!
How charmingly sweet you sing!
O let us be married! too long we have tarried:
But what shall we do for a ring?'
They sailed away for a year and a day,
To the land where the Bong-tree grows
And there in the wood a Piggy-wig stood
With a ring at the end of his nose,
   His nose,
   His nose,
With a ring at the end of his nose.

© Andrew Brodie Publications ✓ www.acblack.com

| YEAR | UNIT | Sheet |
| 2 | 21 | A |

Name: The Owl and the Pussy-cat

Here is the third verse.

'Dear Pig, are you willing to sell for one shilling,
Your ring?' Said the Piggy, 'I will.'
So they took it away and were married next day,
By the turkey who lives on the hill.
They dined on mince, and slices of quince,
Which they ate with a runcible spoon.
And hand in hand, on the edge of the sand,
They danced by the light of the moon,
    The moon,
    The moon,
They danced by the light of the moon.

by Edward Lear

Answer these questions. You may need to read all the verses again.

How long did the Owl and the Pussycat sail away for?

_____

_____

What sort of tree was growing where they landed?

_____

_____

© Andrew Brodie Publications ✓ www.acblack.com

| YEAR 2 | UNIT 21 | Sheet B |

Name: _____   The Owl and the Pussy-cat

Who lived on a hill?

☐ **Piggy-wig**   ☐ **Owl**   ☐ **Pussy-cat**   ☐ **Turkey**

How much did Piggy-wig charge for his ring?

☐ a shilling   ☐ a penny   ☐ a pound   ☐ ten pence

Where did Piggy-wig keep his ring?

☐ his pocket   ☐ his finger   ☐ his neck   ☐ his nose

How many characters are in the poem?

_____

_____

Choose your favourite verse of the poem. Write it in your best handwriting. Practise reading it aloud.

_____

_____

_____

_____

_____

_____

_____

_____

_____

This unit addresses the Literacy Strategy:
Term 1, 2, 3 objective   1: to reinforce and apply their word-level skills through shared and guided reading.
Term 1, 2, 3 objective   2: to use phonological, contextual, grammatical and graphic knowledge to work out, predict, and check the meanings of unfamiliar words and to make sense of what they read.
You may also find it helpful when covering :
Term 2 objective 17: that dictionaries and glossaries give definitions and explanations; discuss what definitions are, explore some simple definitions in dictionaries.
Term 3 objective 15: to use a contents page and index to find way about text.

YEAR 2 | UNIT 22 | Sheet A   Name   Caring for Your Dog

Here is the contents page of Jamie's book.

Use it to help you to answer the questions on the next page.

Caring For Your Dog

Chapter	Page number
Feeding	page 2
Grooming	page 4
Exercise	page 7
Training	page 10
Care of puppies	page 13
Dog shows	page 18
Breeds of dog	page 20
Glossary	page 28
Index	page 32

© Andrew Brodie Publications ✓ www.acblack.com

| YEAR 2 | UNIT 22 | Sheet B |

Name _____ Caring for Your Dog

Write the answers to these questions.

What is the title of the book? ☐

Would you expect to find the contents page near the beginning or the end of the book? ☐

Which chapter of the book would tell you about different types of dog? ☐

Which page would you turn to, to find out what to give your dog to eat? ☐

Which chapter would tell you how to look after a very young dog? ☐

Which chapter would tell you how often to take your dog for a walk? ☐

Which chapter would tell you about brushing your dog? ☐

The glossary is on page 28. What is a glossary?

_____

© Andrew Brodie Publications ✓ www.acblack.com

Key Objectives: to assess pupils' recognition of the essential high frequency words suggested for years 1 and 2.

YEAR	UNIT	Sheet
2	23	A

Brodie's non-standardised contextual word reading assessment for Key Stage One

Teachers' Page

The following story, *Jill's Bad Day*, contains 105 of the words suggested in the Literacy Framework for Years 1 and 2. It also contains 30 of the suggested high frequency words for Reception.

The story is printed once as a comprehension exercise for the child to read, and once with 100 of the Year 1 and 2 target words underlined with a box next to them. This is for you to use as an assessment sheet to record the sight recognition of these high frequency words. We suggest that you simply mark the box for each word that is read correctly. Find the total number of correct words and this will provide you with a percentage score for the test. We suggest that you carry out this assessment twice during the school year, thus enabling you to make a judgement of each individual pupil's progress. You may wish to spread the assessment over two sessions. Please note that some of the target words appear more than once but are only tested once.

Years 1 and 2 words that appear in the story. (Those in brackets are not tested.)

were	name	good	could	do	help	his
lived	after	girl	can't	back	have	just
(an)	came	but	new	home	got	been
old	because	there	(be)	made	that	how
school	too	time	(so)	very	way	many
next	out	when	little	another	take	here
their	first	took	not	will	some	where
house	then	red	your	him	(off)	would
had	about	ball	must	(us)	push	over
sister	twenty	three	one	again	as	by
called	nine	more	blue	don't	night	much
who	put	with	saw	want	two	now
ten	door	her	bed	people	them	than
brother	ran	boy	did	may	should	from
twelve	down	if	what	laugh	make	last

Years 1 and 2 words missing from the story.

half	dig	love	once	our	seen	water
has	jump	man	or	pull	these	

Plus: days, months, numbers to twenty, colours.

30 Reception high frequency words that appear in the story.

and	to	look	up	you	is
they	was	on	it	like	the
in	big	she	go	my	mum
a	he	play	me	I	yes
went	day	said	at	we	no

© Andrew Brodie Publications ✓ www.acblack.com

Year 2 | Unit 23 | Sheet B

Brodie's non-standardised contextual word reading assessment for Key Stage One

Teacher's copy

100 target words for Year 1 and Year 2

Name	Percentage Score
Date	Year Group
Date of Birth	Chronological Age

Jill and Jack <u>were</u> ☐ twins. They <u>lived</u> ☐ in a village and went to an <u>old</u> ☐ <u>school</u> ☐ which was <u>next</u> ☐ to <u>their</u> ☐ <u>house</u>. ☐ They <u>had</u> ☐ a baby <u>sister</u> ☐ <u>called</u> ☐ Lily, <u>who</u> ☐ was <u>ten</u> ☐ months old, and a big <u>brother</u> ☐ who was <u>twelve</u> ☐ years old. His <u>name</u> ☐ was Ben.

Every day <u>after</u> ☐ breakfast their Gran <u>came</u> ☐ to look after Lily <u>because</u> ☐ their Mum went to school <u>too</u>. ☐ She was a teacher. Mum went <u>out</u> ☐ <u>first</u> ☐ and <u>then</u> ☐ at <u>about</u> ☐ <u>twenty</u> ☐ minutes to <u>nine</u> ☐ Jill and Jack <u>put</u> ☐ on their coats, went out through the <u>door</u> ☐ and <u>ran</u> ☐ <u>down</u> ☐ the road to school.

Now, Jill was usually a <u>good</u> ☐ <u>girl</u> ☐ <u>but</u> ☐ today was going to be different. <u>There</u> ☐ was no problem until play <u>time</u>, ☐ <u>when</u> ☐ Jill <u>took</u> ☐ a <u>red</u> ☐ <u>ball</u> ☐ out to play. She chose <u>three</u> ☐ <u>more</u> ☐ children to play <u>with</u> ☐ <u>her</u>, ☐ and then the trouble began.

A <u>boy</u>, ☐ who was only in Year One, asked <u>if</u> ☐ he <u>could</u> ☐ play too.

"No you <u>can't</u>, ☐ it's my <u>new</u> ☐ ball," said Jill crossly.

Just then, Jack came up.

"Don't be so mean," he said. "Let the <u>little</u> ☐ boy play. Anyway it is <u>not</u> ☐ <u>your</u> ☐ ball, it <u>must</u> ☐ be mine because I had the red <u>one</u>. ☐ Your ball is <u>blue</u>. ☐ I <u>saw</u> ☐ it on your <u>bed</u>." ☐

Jill <u>did</u> ☐ not know <u>what</u> ☐ to <u>do</u> ☐ so she went <u>back</u> ☐ <u>home</u>. ☐ Gran called Mum on the telephone and <u>made</u> ☐ Jill say she was <u>very</u> ☐ sorry.

"<u>Another</u> ☐ time I <u>will</u> ☐ let <u>him</u> ☐ play with us," said Jill. "I won't be mean <u>again</u>. ☐ I <u>don't</u> ☐ <u>want</u> ☐ to go back to school because <u>people</u> ☐ <u>may</u> ☐ <u>laugh</u> ☐ at me," she said.

"Don't worry," said Gran. I will <u>help</u> ☐ you. I <u>have</u> ☐ <u>got</u> ☐ to go <u>that</u> ☐ <u>way</u> ☐ to <u>take</u> ☐ <u>some</u> ☐ letters to the post box…. Off we go! You <u>push</u> ☐ Lily <u>as</u> ☐ far as the school."

That <u>night</u> ☐ Mum said that the <u>two</u> ☐ of <u>them</u> ☐ <u>should</u> ☐ <u>make</u> ☐ friends before bed time and Jill should give Jack <u>his</u> ☐ ball.

"Yes, we have made friends," said Jack.

"It has <u>just</u> ☐ <u>been</u> ☐ a bad day," sighed Jill, "I won't mind <u>how</u> ☐ <u>many</u> ☐ people play ball next time. <u>Here</u> ☐ is your red ball, Jack. <u>Where</u> ☐ <u>would</u> ☐ you like me to put it?"

"<u>Over</u> ☐ <u>by</u> ☐ my bag please," replied Jack.

"I feel <u>much</u> ☐ better <u>now</u> ☐ <u>than</u> ☐ I did at school," said Jill as she got up <u>from</u> ☐ the chair. "That is the very <u>last</u> ☐ time I stop being good!"

Mum just smiled.

© Andrew Brodie Publications ✓ www.acblack.com

Jill's Bad Day

Jill and Jack were twins. They lived in a village and went to an old school which was next to their house. They had a baby sister called Lily, who was ten months old, and a big brother who was twelve years old. His name was Ben.

Every day after breakfast their Gran came to look after Lily because their Mum went to school too. She was a teacher. Mum went out first and then, at about twenty minutes to nine, Jill and Jack put on their coats, went out through the door and ran down the road to school.

Now, Jill was usually a good girl but today was going to be different. There was no problem until play time, when Jill took a red ball out to play. She chose three more children to play with her, and then the trouble began. A boy, who was only in Year One, asked if he could play too.

"No you can't, it's my new ball," said Jill crossly. Just then, Jack came up.

"Don't be so mean," he said. "Let the little boy

play. Anyway it's not your ball, it must be mine because I had the red one. Your ball is blue. I saw it on your bed."

Jill did not know what to do so she went back home.

Gran called Mum on the telephone and made Jill say she was very sorry.

"Another time I will let him play with us," said Jill. "I won't be mean again. I don't want to go back to school because people may laugh at me," she said.

"Don't worry," said Gran. "I will help you. I have got to go that way to take some letters to the post box.... Off we go! You push Lily as far as the school."

That night Mum said that the two of them should make friends before bed time and Jill should give Jack his ball.

"Yes, we have made friends," said Jack.

"It has just been a bad day," sighed Jill, "I won't mind how many people play ball next time. Here is your red ball, Jack. Where would you like me to put it?"

"Over by my bag please," replied Jack.

"I feel much better now than I did at school," said Jill as she got up from the chair. "That is the very last time I stop being good!"

Mum just smiled.

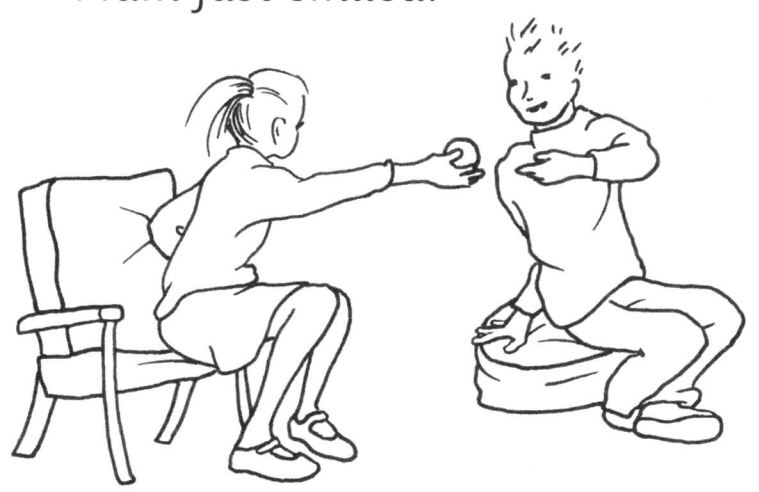

Jill did the wrong thing by going home. Remember it is not safe to go out of school on your own.

| YEAR 2 | UNIT 23 | Sheet E |

Name _____   Jill's' Bad day

Jill's Bad Day

1. In the story how many children were in Jill and Jack's family altogether?

    1 ☐   2 ☐   3 ☐   4 ☐

2. Who looked after baby Lily each day?
   Draw a ring round the correct answer.

   (Mum)   (Gran)   (Ben)   (Jill)

3. What colour was the ball Jill took out to play?

   _____

   _____

4. Where did Jack say he had seen Jill's blue ball?

   _____

   _____

5. Fill in the missing words:

   Gran called ☐ on the telephone and

   then Jill said she was ☐.

   Gran walked back to school with ☐

   because she had some ☐ to put in

   the post box. Gran said Jill could ☐

   Lily as far ☐ the school.

© Andrew Brodie Publications ✓ www.acblack.com

| YEAR 2 | UNIT 23 | Sheet F | Name | Jill's Bad Day |

6. Jill should not have left school.
What do you think Jill should have done instead of going home?

_____
_____
_____
_____

abcdefghijklmnopqrstuvwxyz

Alphabetical Order

Put the following lists of words in alphabetical order.

(a) girl   about   down   could   must

(b) off   house   just   may   should

(c) twenty   people   school   three   where

(d) little   from   after   an   got

(e) take   ball   could   back   people

abcdefghijklmnopqrstuvwxyz

© Andrew Brodie Publications ✓ www.acblack.com